Carving on Porta della Pescheria, Modena Cathedral (See page 20)

Arthur of Albion

AN INTRODUCTION TO
THE ARTHURIAN LITERATURE
AND LEGENDS OF ENGLAND

BY

R. W. BARBER

WITH A FOREWORD BY
DAVID JONES

BARNES & NOBLE, INC. • NEW YORK

PUBLISHERS • BOOKSELLERS • FOUNDED 1873

CONTENTS

FOREWORD

IN attempting a brief foreword to Mr. Barber's study I must first make it plain that I do so in a purely amateur capacity. I do not write as a scholar but rather as a person whose own work has, in various ways and over the years, been not uninfluenced by a feeling for this material.

His book, so it appears to me on a first reading of it, is a well thought out, unassuming and clear account of this involved matter—the *matière de Bretagne*, especially as it has come down to us through English channels.

The Arthurian deposits are not only, of their own nature, highly complex, but have been further complicated by bias, by unequal scholarship and by that counterfeit of Imagination and her worst enemy, whimsy: a thing corruptive alike to artist and scholar.

So that, one way or another, it has, in the past, been none too easy for most readers to obtain a reliable report on the geology of Arthuriania. I use this term with deliberation, because a geological analogy best suits the case. There are the sedimented strata laid down on earlier strata, there are the intrusive rocks thrust up from fires long since dead, there are the inversions and the faultings, there are the strange erratics brought by flows from very far off, there are the recent deposits and there is metamorphosis, and pseudomorphosis as well.

Such then is the formidable character of the mass of material which Mr. Barber has chosen for his study.

It seems to me that in so doing he has, however accidentally, provided the general reader and the student also with one of the best accounts of how this matter stands to-day.

I would emphasize *to-day*, because the findings of the authorities consulted by any writer on this subject are, to this or that degree, interim findings. Fragments of fresh information, sometimes coming from quite unexpected sources and from quite other fields of research, continue to filter in.

Only the other day, in a broadcast, Mr. Arthur Waley drew our attention to the employment, in an early mediaeval Chinese romance, of the motif of the entwined trees sprung from the graves of the lovers, exactly as we have it in the Arthurian romance of Iseult and her lover. A mere coincidental detail you may think, but an illuminating one and from very far afield.

Kipling's East is East and West is West does not apply to the Arthurian complex. Nor should this surprise us, for there is, after all, but one tale to tell: *Dilectus meus mihi, et ego illi*, as *The Canticle of Canticles* puts it.

That is, so long as we remember that in that one tale is comprised the mutual love of God and man, of lord and vassal, of battle-mate and battle-mate, as well as the love of Launcelot and Guenever, of Gareth and Liones. Nor should we forget the frustrated love of Palomides, though in that case there was no *Dilectus meus*, or should I say no *et ego illi*? I'm not sure.

It may appear that I am wandering far from the object of this foreword, which is to recommend Mr. Barber's book. But if I meander it is in order to indicate something of the tangled and meandering nature of the material with which he has had to cope.

You will get nowhere with this material unless you approach it obliquely. It is only by patient infiltrations that you will begin to understand the many and varied aspects of this thing. It is always a matter of 'before and before again'.

As we all know, the salient characteristic of the figure of Arthur himself is that he will 'come again out of Faerie'.

The notion that it was futile to seek the grave of Arthur is expressed in one of the earliest of Welsh remains, in a verse from the *Englynion y Beddau* (Stanzas of the Graves). And we all know the words which are supposed to have been inscribed on his imagined tomb at Glastonbury: *Hic jacet Arthurus rex quondam rexque futurus.*

Well, here is Mr. Barber's study to show that even to-day, when journeys to Venus seem just round the corner and when most of us are haunted by the uncreaturely shape of things to come, and have little heart for what has made us, a young writer can apply himself to a careful analysis of the Arthurian material, so that it may live again in our minds, thereby recalling the Springtime of the West.

One of the merits of this study is that while it is in that good tradition of scholarship which demands relevant references for statements made, yet it is not pedantic or tedious. I should mention the appendices, which collate much diverse material.

I would not suggest that there is nothing to criticise; there are matters of omission, of emphasis and of detail which may be queried, but such is not my function here.

It is heartening to remember that this is the book of a writer who is but on the threshold of his life's work.

In conclusion, I would relate how only yesterday, a friend of mine, finding her child in tears and supposing him to be unwell, discovered that his grief was occasioned by the reading of a child's popular version of what is called in Malory, 'the moste pyteous tale of the Morte Arthur Saunz Gwerdon'.

For this child, at least, the spell still holds: and they say that children can father men.

March 1961   DAVID JONES

PREFACE

'WHAT place is there within the bounds of the empire of Christendom to which the winged praise of Arthur the Briton has not extended? Who is there, I ask, who does not speak of Arthur the Briton, since he is but little less known to the peoples of Asia than to the Bretons, as we are informed by pilgrims who return from Eastern lands? The peoples of the East speak of him as do those of the West, though separated by the breadth of the whole earth. Egypt speaks of him, nor is the Bosphorus silent. Rome, queen of cities, sings his deeds, and his wars are known to her former rival, Carthage. Antioch, Armenia and Palestine celebrate his feats.'

No British hero has ever had a higher reputation abroad than King Arthur, as the twelfth-century writer Alanus de Insulis tells us in the passage above. But although Arthur enjoyed great glory abroad, and an extensive following, it is at home that this fame has endured longest. The Arthurian legend recurs throughout our literature from the twelfth to the twentieth century, and has inspired three of our greatest masterpieces: *Sir Gawain and the Green Knight*, Sir Thomas Malory's eight noble tales, and Tennyson's poems, as well as much other superb poetry and prose. But in tracing its course many problems are involved, for the stream is by no means continuous. We have to account not only for the times when Arthur was held in esteem, but also for those when his name was forgotten, only to reappear in new splendour.

Yet no straightforward introduction to this major force in our
literature has been written for the general reader. It is hoped that
the present book will provide such a guide. And, having traced
Arthur's progress from his place in history to his appearances in
modern poetry, we can begin to suggest the answers to such larger
problems as the reason for Arthur's popularity today, and his
special validity to the modern writer.

Since the subject is such a complex one, more references than
would be usual in a general work have been given to allow the
reader to investigate any particular branch that may interest him.
Also, because of the obscurity of some of the legends, summaries
of many works have been provided, though it is assumed that the
reader will know the very broadest outline of Arthur's career as
found in Malory or Tennyson.

ACKNOWLEDGEMENTS

THIS book was the result of a Trevelyan scholarship project, and was written in its original form at Marlborough College. The writer would like to thank those who gave him encouragement in the early stages of the work, especially Mr. G. W. Murray, Mr. R. Ockenden, and Mr. P. N. Carter. He must also acknowledge the patience of the librarians of Wiltshire and Essex County Libraries in satisfying his requests for unusual and rare books, not all of which have been included in the bibliography, and the kindness of the authorities of the Taylorian Institute, Oxford, in allowing him to consult various scholarly periodicals.

ARTHUR OF ALBION

ONE

THE UNKNOWN COMMANDER

THE first questions that most people interested in King Arthur ask are: Did he really exist? Who was he? And we must obviously know something about him and his place in history before we discuss his literary roles. Again, we may wonder what it was that made the British people remember him for six hundred years after his time, and why an historian then exalted his name until he rivalled Charlemagne in splendour and realms. The answers to such dramatic questions are matters of doubt and confusion; for the period of Arthur's life is one of the most obscure in our history. Hence we cannot say very much about either his character or his career. Nor can we possibly supply the missing information by identifying him with some other, better-known historical person, as has occasionally been attempted on very slender evidence. But, even though we know there can be no clear answer, the riddle is fascinating in itself.

Britain in the fifth century A.D. was in process of undergoing one of the most protracted and radical periods of transition in its history. The order imposed by the Romans was already crumbling when the legions withdrew about 410; already the towns were declining, and the magnates lived in villas around them, largely free from the crushing burden of taxation imposed by the complex bureaucracy. The withdrawal of the troops in fact led to an increase in prosperity, since these taxes were now removed.

B   I

It is believed that the troops may have returned in small numbers and with a rather less complex administration between 417 and 427, but the pattern of post-Roman Britain was evolving regardless of their presence.

This pattern has much to do with Arthur. The Roman power was distributed among a number of small magnates, and a struggle developed between these local leaders. By 440 several kingdoms seem to have formed, consisting of a loose overlordship in civil and military matters. At this stage, one of these kings, Vortigern, troubled by the Picts, invited the Saxons to Britain to deal with them, and found that he had exchanged a minor difficulty for a major one. The Saxons soon rose against him, and were in effective control of the eastern half of the island by the last decade of the century.

But this description may give a false impression of two sharply-divided racial camps, each with its own leader. In fact, neither side was in the least unified. The Saxons were grouped in war-bands, each under its own leader; these might unite for a brief time, but would soon range off on their own to plunder and ravage. The settled population of eastern England, such as it was, must have remained largely British for two or three decades, owing no allegiance to Saxon lords, but merely being their almost defenceless prey. On the other side, the Britons had some sort of organized resistance, as is shown by the huge earthworks dating from around this period. We know from them and from other archaeological evidence that the main Saxon incursions were up the Thames valley, along the East Coast and inland from the Fens, and along the South Coast. Their general advance was checked about 490 by a British force led by Aurelius Ambrosius, but their war-bands continued to make inroads into British territory.

Possibly in reaction against the unwieldy Roman organizations, British life during the century became more and more pastoral. This is seen from the methods of defence, among other evidence. Instead of relying on retreating into the security of the walled towns (the Saxons very rarely captured these), hill-forts and dykes were built and renewed, while the towns diminished in size and importance. Yet there remained some form of administration, and trade continued to the end of the century. The culture of the Romans was gradually forgotten, though it would seem that some of the leading families still looked to Rome as the centre of civilization.[1]

Such is the scene against which Arthur's figure appears. Few writers were at hand to describe it; in fact we have only three historical or moral works which portray the struggle from the point of view of the Britons of the century after it. And none of them yields a coherent picture of Arthur himself. The first of these, Gildas, a Welsh monk who probably lived near Glastonbury composed his *De Excidio Britanniae*,[2] sometimes known as the 'Liber Querolus' or 'Book of Complaints', about fifty years after the period that interests us. He is, however, less concerned with the recent past than with the present, and the majority of his book is a virulent attack on his British contemporaries. In the course of this jeremiad, he mentions many distinguished Romans and Britons of the preceding century—but not Arthur. In his brief introductory history, he chronicles British fortunes from the departure of the Romans up to the exploits of Aurelius Ambrosius, and finishes:

> 'And now his progeny in these our days, although shamefully degenerated from the worthiness of their ancestors, provoke to battle their cruel conquerors, and by the goodness of the Lord obtain the victory.
> 'After this, sometimes our countrymen, sometimes the enemy, won the field, . . . until the year of the siege of mons Badonus, when took place almost the last and not the least slaughter of our cruel foes.'[3]

A rather confused passage follows, which seems to be best interpreted as dating the siege of mons Badonus forty-four years before the time at which he was writing, that being also the year

in which he was born. Other writers, however, among them
Bede, who must have used a text at least three hundred years
older than any we possess, interpret it as forty-four years after
the coming of the Saxons. In either case, the date of the siege
cannot be fixed accurately. If the first reading is correct, the cal-
culation will be as follows: since we know from Welsh and Irish
annals that Gildas died in about 570 and wrote not later than
547, probably c. 540, the siege of mons Badonus is unlikely to
have been earlier than 490 or later than 503.[4] If Bede is correct,
we will have to fix the date of the coming of the Saxons—a problem that will probably never be solved. At the moment, around
440 is the favoured date, assuming that he means the first major
incursion and not an isolated raid. This would fix the date of
Badon at about 485–90.

We also learn from Gildas that this victory was followed by a
lengthy period of peace. The Saxons, seeing that no further
plunder was to be had, turned to the business of settlement; this,
at any rate, would explain why the Britons were almost un-
molested for forty years, and is confirmed by archaeological evidence. But if such a great breathing-space was won at Badon,
why does Gildas not tell us the name of the leader of the British
in this battle? We have to explain why this leader should be identified with Arthur; and this record of the victory written within
living memory of it which fails to mention him is no light obstacle. Fortunately it is not our only record.

The first theory proposed to cover this omission is of great
age. Caradoc of Llancarfan, in his *Life of Gildas*,* written in the
eleventh century, mentions a feud between Arthur and Gildas.[5]
Here Arthur is supposed to have killed Gildas's brother, the
King of Brittany, and Gildas makes him do penance for the
crime. However, such biographies are rarely historical; often the
idea behind them is that the greater the rank of the sinner forced
to repent, the greater the glory of the saint. But reference to Gildas's own work will destroy this story, unsupported as it is. If

* Gildas was a saint of the Celtic Church.

Arthur was a successful commander nearing the end of his career at mons Badonus, in the year that Gildas was born, they would never have met on such terms.

The real clue lies elsewhere. There are two obvious factors which led Gildas to omit all reference to Arthur. At this point we may discount all oblique references or nicknames, since there is already ample evidence without resorting to conundrums. Firstly, we can tell from Gildas's tone throughout that he favoured what remained of the Roman party in Britain, looking back to the days of the Roman occupation as a 'Golden Age' of peace and justice, and to the Roman commanders as models of energy and courage. Anything connected with Rome is never criticized. On the other hand, Gildas proclaims on every page his contempt for the Britons of his day, especially their rulers. He attacks the entire nation for their slothfulness in battle and contrasts them with his ideal, the Romans. The third part of his work, the so-called 'Epistle',[6] opens with his bitterest attack: 'Britain has kings, but they are tyrants: judges, but they are unrighteous, usually engaged in plunder and rapine, for ever preying on the innocent . . .' He sums up the indictment thus: '. . . they are the proud, murderers, this and adulterers too, enemies of God who should be totally destroyed'. We can hardly expect him to indulge in panegyrics on Arthur, for this is his usual tone throughout the book.

But this does not preclude a chance mention, which we would rightly hope to find. There is a better and apparently overlooked answer in the preface,[7] where he specifically declares that his object is 'to relate the deeds of a slothful and indolent race rather than the exploits of those who have been successful in the field'. This would seem to imply quite clearly that he had omitted references to military affairs as far as possible, and this is borne out by the rest of the book. Naturally Arthur, assuming him to be the unknown commander of mons Badonus, would be the most likely person to suffer from this decision. And even should this be considered an insufficient excuse, we can always fall back on Gildas's reluctance to mention personal names.

So far we have merely shown that around 490 a great battle was fought at mons Badonus, or Mount Badon, and that the commander of the victorious British troops is unknown, but could possibly be Arthur. The earliest evidence which points to him as the missing figure dates from about a century later. In the early Welsh poem *Gododdin*[8] (whose author is believed to be the poet Aneirin), written *c.* 600, a hero called Arthur is recorded, and we may deduce that he was famous around this time. It is said of one warrior that 'he glutted the black ravens (with the bodies of his enemies), although he was no Arthur'. Unfortunately, parts of this poem were added at a later date, and it cannot be proved that this is not one of them. If this remark did indeed date from the end of the sixth century, it would considerably strengthen our case, showing as it does Arthur's name as a byword for heroic actions. But there is another factor which does almost this. About 550–600, the hitherto unknown name Arthur appears in British records. It then disappears again almost immediately. One conclusion we can draw is that some heroic figure among the Britons must have been so named; and that boys had been named after him, in the same way that many a boy born in the early decades of the nineteenth century bore the name Horatio because of Nelson's exploits. And this is confirmed by the knowledge that a Scottish king, Aedan mac Gabrain, christened one of his sons Arthur at this same time because he hoped he would head a campaign to drive the English out of Northumbria.

For all this jumble of incidental evidence we have only a heroic, nameless commander, and the name of a hero whose exploits are unknown. As yet, to identify the two as the same man would be useless. But so far we have examined only one of the three accounts of the period. We must now turn to the second, a chronicle compiled in the early ninth century, three hundred years later than the actual events. It is the work of one Nennius, again, like Gildas, a Welsh monk. Here we have a whole paragraph on Arthur; but we can only guess as to where this came from. The nature of what is said about him has given rise to one plausible suggestion.[9] Nennius gives a catalogue of confused battle-names in prose, numbering twelve. Now poems which list exploits in the form of such catalogues of names are by no means uncommon in Welsh literature of the period, and Nennius may easily have used such a work. How old the traditions it embodies are we cannot tell. None the less, what he has to say is of great importance:

> 'In those days the Saxons grew in numbers and prospered in Britain. But at Hengist's death, Octha his son came from the western parts of the island to the kingdom of Kent. Then Arthur and the kings of the Britons fought against them, but Arthur himself was leader in the battles. The first battle was at the mouth of the river called Glein; the second, third, fourth and fifth on another river, which is called Dubglas, in the region Linnuis. The sixth battle was on the river known as Bassas. The seventh was in the forest of Celidon, that is to say, Cat Coit Celidon. In the eighth battle at Castle Guinnion, Arthur bore upon his shoulders the image of Mary, the Holy Virgin; the heathen were put to flight that day, and through the might of our Lord Jesus Christ there was a great slaughter of them. The ninth battle took place at the City of Legions. The tenth battle was waged on the banks of the river Tribroit. The eleventh battle was fought on the mountain called Agned. At the twelfth battle on Mount Badon, there fell in one day nine hundred and sixty men under one onslaught of Arthur's men, and none conquered save he alone, and in all the battles he was victor.'*

Here Arthur has become a definite historical character. He is the chosen 'dux bellorum', having the whole British chieftaincy

* See Appendix for variations in text.

under him. Apparently he leads them twelve times in all, winning every battle. These battles are the first details of his career
that we possess, and have been the subject of much argument. It
is therefore worth considering the various theories that have
been based on them, although these are highly controversial and
little hard fact has emerged from the discussion.

These theories are mainly concerned with the geographical
area in which Arthur fought. Four regions especially have figured
in these arguments: the Scottish border and Strathclyde, Wales,
the East Coast, and Wessex; and the names of the battles have
been interpreted to fit the region favoured. Very few of the
twelve sites named can be even approximately placed on modern
maps.

The first battle, at the mouth of the river Glein, has been attributed to Northumberland, Lincolnshire, and Sussex. The subsequent series of four battles on the Dubglas river in Linnuis is
probably the result of some writer's memory of a tradition about
Arthur's twelve battles: finding he only had nine names, he had
to resort to this multiple combat. As to the names, Dubglas
means Blackwater, and is as common a river name as Avon in its
various forms. Linnuis is undoubtedly Lindsey; but there is no
river corresponding to Dubglas in Lindsey. The site of the sixth,
on the Bassas (or Lusas, as another reliable manuscript has it)
has not yet found an even remotely satisfactory modern equivalent. The seventh, 'in Cat Coit Celidon', is probably connected
with the 'silva Caledoniae'; but this in itself seems to have
covered most of the northern forests. Castle Guinnion, the
eighth on the list, is definitely one of the Roman camps whose
name begins in Bini- or Vini-, but these are well scattered
throughout England.

The incident told in connection with this battle is of an image
of the Virgin carried by Arthur which aided him in defeating the
heathens. But this detail almost certainly belongs to the Mount
Badon encounter, as we shall see from the third of our three
sources for this period, the *Annales Cambriae*.

At first sight, the ninth battle seems to be easy of solution, for City of Legion invariably means Chester in Welsh texts; yet the Saxons had not reached that point in Arthur's day. There was a much greater battle there in 616, and it is possible that this later fight has crept in by mistake. No modern equivalent has been found for Tribroit, although it occurs elsewhere in Welsh literature. Edinburgh has been put forward as the site of the eleventh, and the local tradition of the hill called Arthur's Seat cited in support. But Edinburgh derives from a very dissimilar British name, Dineiddin, which could hardly be corrupted to 'Agned'.

Finally, there is mons Badonus itself. This is the only unquestionably genuine combat in the entire list. Gildas and Nennius agree in describing it as the last great victory over the Saxons, and if it could only be proved to be one of the half-dozen sites suggested, Arthur could be given a physical background which he totally lacks as an historical figure. However, the choice is not too wide. The area in which Badon lies is almost certainly around Bath and the Severn estuary, and not further east than Salisbury. Badbury near Swindon (Liddington Castle), Badbury Hill near Faringdon, and Badbury Rings near Blandford are the most important candidates. We have already considered its date.

What conclusions can we draw from this? Firstly, that most of the account is quite unreliable; the battles, even if genuine, may not have been fought by Arthur, with the solitary exception of Badon. As to theories supporting any one part of England based on them alone, they are totally unreliable. We can produce a little evidence, however. From the known position of the Saxons at Arthur's time, the South, and especially the region bordering the Thames valley would be most likely. Some theories that he was northern in origin are seriously discounted by the absence of the Picts from all accounts of his campaigns. Only in legends far too late to have any historical value do they appear as his enemies. We mentioned as a possible source for Nennius's account a chronicle-poem cataloguing Arthur's victories. It is possible that the compiler of this confused several people in his

account of Arthur: one may have been a late defender of the
Roman Wall, thus providing such northern influence as there is;
the second a Count of the Saxon Shore, the official responsible
during the Roman occupation for the defence of the East Coast
against the inroads of the Scandinavian and Germanic tribes;
and finally the defender of the West of England and victor of
Badon, the real Arthur. It was in this region that he was best remembered, and here that the Saxons met with the first firm
British resistance.

Two remarks in this early record of Arthur tell us little more
about his historical character, but provided great opportunities
for later writers. The first is found in two variants of Nennius:
'Then Arthur and the kings of the Britons fought against them
[i.e. the Saxons]; and though there were many more noble than
he, he was twelve times chosen commander and won the battles.'

Here we have one possible reason why the story of his concealed birth and eventual recognition as heir to the throne was
invented by later writers.[10] As pretended historians, they would
probably have known this account, and could not afford to con-
tradict it directly. To avoid having to reduce the status of their
hero, they invented the story of transformation and tragedy we
shall discuss later.

The last of our three sources, which has already been quoted
in reference to the battle of Badon, is the *Annales Cambriae*, an
anonymous list of important dates in Welsh history, of the early
ninth century. Arthur is mentioned twice. Under A.D. 516 we
read: 'Battle of Badon in which Arthur carried the cross of our
Lord Jesus Christ on his shoulders three nights and days, and
the Britons were victorious.' This is apparently a recollection of
a story similar to that in Nennius. The dating of the battle, about
fifteen years later than Gildas is probably affected by a chronological miscalculation, since all its dates are similarly inaccurate.
It is the second entry that is really interesting. '537: Arthur and
Medraut fell at Camlann: and many died in Britain and Ireland . . .' This is not an historical witness to Arthur's death in

civil war; but it lengthens his recorded life by twenty years after his great military triumph, and thus gave the romancers admirable opportunity to set to work without contradicting the known facts; if challenged by more serious historians, they could point to this gap, and ask for a better explanation. And in the reference itself lies the nucleus of the 'last dim battle in the West' which was later to become so integral a part of the tragedy of Arthur. Here also lies the historical basis for the character of Mordred. Had we lost all traces of Arthur after Mount Badon, the romances might have run very differently.

Before concluding our portrait of the historical Arthur, we may well ask how he succeeded in defeating the Saxons so decisively, with no military tradition or training behind him. It may have been sheer energy and organizational and tactical ability: but one very attractive explanation has been offered, which would make such a victory more plausible. Arthur's name, with its probable origin in the Roman family name Artorius, would imply that he came of at least partly Roman blood, and it is argued that he may well have known something of Roman civilization, and, as a military leader, something of their tactics and equipment. Certainly some forty years earlier, the leaders of the opposition to Vortigern had looked to Gaul for help and inspiration, and the evidence of trade shows that the links between Britain and Gaul were still considerable in Arthur's period. Now we know that in Gaul cataphracts, a Byzantine form of heavily-armed cavalry, had been used successfully against the barbarian invaders. In Britain, too, the defence of the East Coast was, in the later years of the Roman occupation, mainly dependent on cavalry, which outnumbered the infantry used here by two to one. Either of these two cavalry forces may have given Arthur the idea of forming a small and extremely mobile band of horsemen, relying for their armour and weapons on such British craftsmen as remained. Such a band would be able to combine with local levies and would explain why Arthur was remembered, not only in the region around the upper Thames and Severn but also much further afield, for with such a mobile force, he might well have fought almost anywhere in Britain. And the mysterious remark of Nennius that at Badon 'there died in one day 960 men under one onslaught of Arthur's men, and none conquered save he alone', might easily mean that this last battle was fought by Arthur's horsemen alone, unsupported by local infantry. Although it is only conjecture, the picture of Arthur's men surprised and trapped in a hill-fort by the Saxons, and fighting their way out to an overwhelming victory by a dramatic charge of cavalry down its steep sides, would help to explain why his name lingered on for so long in the minds and stories of the Welsh.[11]

We can only sketch in the barest outlines of Arthur's historical character and career on such scant evidence; but some sort of figure does emerge from the prejudice and confusion of our earliest writers. One of the last Britons with Roman connections, he was probably born in the third quarter of the fifth century, not long after the arrival of the Saxons in force. By the time he became commander, most of eastern England was dominated by them, and their war-bands were attempting to loot such prizes as remained in the West, swarming up the river valleys; but under his command, and possibly through a cavalry force formed by him, they were decisively overthrown in a campaign or series of isolated battles, which ended with the great victory at Badon about 490. The Saxons, realizing the superiority of the Britons, ceased their attacks until after his death, when internal struggles, of which Gildas was a witness, broke up the temporary unity created under Arthur's leadership. Arthur himself died some twenty years after Badon, probably in battle. Such was the unknown commander; and from memories of him and of the last period of prosperity the Britons enjoyed, was to spring the image of a far better chronicled, but hardly greater, hero, the Arthur of literature.

TWO

FROM REALITY TO ROMANCE

FOR some seven centuries after Arthur won his great victory, his name vanishes into the mists. A little can be gleaned about him from the historians whose accounts we have considered; but even less emerges from the Welsh poets and story-tellers. This is partly because we possess only the fragmentary remains of Welsh literature; but even here the appearances of Arthur are all too infrequent and mysterious. The only reference to his military prowess, in Aneirin's *Gododdin*, has already been quoted; elsewhere the poets have made of him a completely legendary figure. Even if we had more of the literature of the Celtic races of Wales, Cornwall and Brittany, we should learn little more about the historical Arthur: but we might understand better how he entered the realms of romance.

As it is, the remnants of the work of the Welsh bards yield nothing more than tantalizing hints at what may have been a considerable body of stories. Nennius, whose account of Arthur's battles is our main source for the historical Arthur, tells us something about the legendary Arthur in the *Mirabilia* (Marvels) attached to his chronicle.[1] Among these episodes there are two which connect Arthur with place-names. At Carn Cabal, he says, which lies in the region of Buelt (Breconshire), there is a stone bearing the footprint of Arthur's hound Cabal while he hunted the boar Troit. This story is found again in a twelfth-century

collection of stories, the *Mabinogi*, as one of the main incidents
of a tale called *Kulhwch and Olwen*, where Arthur and his followers pursue the magical boar 'Twrch Troit'. It sounds as
though this hunt was already an heroic theme in Nennius's
day.

Elsewhere in the same work is an account of the grave of
Arthur's son Amr. This tomb, in the region of Erging (Hereford-
shire), may be measured as often as anyone cares to do it, but the
result will never be the same as before. However, it is not this,
but how Amr met his death, that interests us; for Nennius says
that he was killed by Arthur, his father. This unpleasant incident
is quite foreign to our modern idea of Arthur. We tend to think
of him as a paragon of chivalry; but in this we are betrayed by
the influence of later English and French writers, for this was
never the view of the Welsh themselves. We shall find a similar,
and to us uncharacteristic, tendency in the *Life of St. Cadoc*; for
just as the chivalric romancers reflect to some extent the times in
which they wrote, so these Welsh legends, of a cruder and less
civilized vein, and more direct in their statements, attributed to
Arthur the morals of their contemporaries. But some of the incidents in which his character is blackened are due to a deliberate
desire to contrast him unfavourably with some saint or other on
the part of the latter's biographers, and hence do not always
represent the real opinion of the times on Arthur.

Indeed, Arthur's roles in Welsh legend vary from the ideal to
the criminal: but the emphasis is usually on the favourable side.
On two occasions he appears as leader of a band of heroic
warriors, a picture of him which was later to lead to his becoming a *roi fainéant* in the romances, who stayed at his court while
his knights performed great deeds. Indeed, in our first poem,
there is nothing to suggest an active role on his part; but it is
only a fragment. It is one of an early thirteenth-century collection, the *Black Book of Carmarthen*; but it was probably written
in the early eleventh century.[2] Arthur is speaking to his door-
keeper about his company of knights. Among them are many

heroes who appear only in Welsh literature; but two are immediately familiar, Cai and Bedwyr, or Kay and Bedivere, in Malory's spelling. The poem breaks off before anything actually happens.

Our second poem, however, does assign to Arthur an active role as leader. It is the thirtieth in the *Book of Taliessin*, another collection of about the year 1200, entitled *The Spoils of Annwfn*.[3] Here Arthur leads an expedition to a Celtic 'Other-world', an earthly realm occupied by supernatural beings, full of strange and magical riches. He sets out with enough warriors to fill his ship 'Pridwen' seven times, apparently with the object of fetching a magic cauldron from this realm, and returns with only seven men. Again, the poem is incomplete, and we hear of only a few of his adventures. But the idea of an expedition to fetch a magical cauldron recurs in *Kulhwch and Olwen*[4] in a more natural form, for here the cauldron belongs to the High Steward of the King of Ireland. This poem is rather later than *The Spoils of Annwfn*, but we have it complete, and it is a fairly long romance. Although it dates from between 1100 and 1130, that is to say, the period when Breton poets were beginning to introduce French ideas into the romances, its conception and contents are pure Welsh. The plot centres round the wooing and winning of Olwen, a giant's daughter, by Kulhwch, Arthur's nephew. To gain her hand, he has to carry out a series of seemingly impossible tasks. The names of the heroes come from earlier Welsh works, but with skilful adaptations where necessary. For instance, the hunting of the boar Troit, the main episode of the poem, has been modernized in such a way as to make it possible for us even now to trace on a map the course followed by Arthur and his men in their pusuit. It covers large areas of Ireland, South Wales and Devon, so carefully described that the story-teller must have known them personally.

As a whole the romance is one of the most attractive of the so-called Mabinogion stories; it has a strongly Celtic and epic flavour in the long recitals of persons and deeds, refreshingly different from the French romances and their derivatives. We now know that it was written without foreign influence, for all the names can be found in earlier Welsh works, while almost entirely absent from the almost contemporary *Historia Regum Britanniae* of Geoffrey of Monmouth. The only other possible derivation from this work, a speech portraying Arthur as a world-renowned conqueror, has a closer parallel in Irish literature.[5] But we could forgive any such minor borrowing, for the rich fantasy of the Celtic imagination in marvels and adventures in this poem is unique and unrivalled; this is the most truly romantic of all Arthur's adventures.

Another genre peculiar to Welsh literature yields more references to Arthur than the poetry, but by its very nature sets more problems than it solves. This is the triad: a group of three connected people, incidents, or things, used as an *aide-memoire* by the bardic story-tellers, so that, having finished one story, they could lead on without hesitation to the next. Unfortunately only these 'headlines' have been preserved, and they are rarely more than half a dozen lines in length. Hence we gather little more about the legendary figure of Arthur from them, although there is no shortage of triads that include him.[6] But other characters whom we shall meet later in the romances make their first appearance here. Two triads mention Guinevere, his wife. One, indeed, tells of the three Guineveres, all apparently wedded to him in turn. This story, that Arthur had more than one wife named Guinevere, was to reappear when, in 1193, Arthur's body was supposedly exhumed with that of Guinevere, '*uxore sua secunda*', his second wife.[7] Again, in the Middle English poem, *Arthour and Merlin*,[8] we meet the true and false Guineveres who are confused with each other at intervals by Arthur. Another triad connects Mordred with Guinevere for the first time; Mordred is said to have raided Arthur's court in Cornwall in one of the *Three Disastrous Expeditions*, dragged Guinevere from her chair and struck her. This resulted in the battle of Camlann, in which both Arthur and Mordred fell. Another version of the same triad says that he committed adultery with her, but this was probably written down after the French writers had made Guinevere's lascivious nature well known.

Of the characters less intimately connected with Arthur himself, three are present in the triads. Tristram and Iseult appear, under the names of Drustan mab Tallwch and Essyllt. Tristram himself was probably an historical Pictish king of the end of the eighth century, Drust.[9] Essyllt is not specifically connected with him, but appears in the same triad. Merchyon, better known to us as King Mark of Cornwall, Iseult's husband, is also mentioned here. Another minor hero of the romances, Ywain, of whom we shall have more to say later, is known in the triads as Owein ap Urien; we have reason to believe that he too was an historical prince of northern origin of the sixth century, absorbed into literature in much the same way as Arthur.

Other Welsh poems which need not concern us for the moment are those about Myrddin, on whom our stories about Merlin are largely based. We find in these fragments another son of Arthur's beside Amr, Lacheu; but he vanishes again except in John Masefield's version of the legend.

The portrait of the Welsh legendary Arthur is even less clearly outlined than that of the historical Arthur. But we have strong evidence for a considerable body of stories centred round him, and this is strengthened when we turn to the biographies of Celtic saints written in Latin in the tenth and eleventh centuries. These, though usually of no literary or historical significance except to the student of saints' lives, contain several references to Arthur which are of interest in that they add some definite stories to support the idea of a current group of traditions concerning him.

The first two stories are to be found in the *Life of St. Cadoc*, the work of one Lifric of Llancarfan. The original version is dated at about 1075,[10] but there may have been later additions. Arthur is once again in an unusual role that is not exactly chivalric; in fact, were it not for the description '*tres heroes strenui*'

C

applied to himself and his two knights, the author might well
have regarded him as an ordinary petty tyrant. He is first seen
playing dice with Kay and Bedivere on a hill-top. A local nobleman appears, eloping with his beloved, whose relatives are in hot
pursuit. Arthur, seized with desire for the girl, proposes to carry
her off himself, but his companions reprimand him, saying that
it is their custom to help the distressed. He is immediately re-
pentant, and all three hold the pursuers at bay, thus allowing the
lovers to escape in safety. He reappears later in the book in a
quarrel over the blood compensation for three of his men who
have been killed. St. Cadoc acts as mediator, but Arthur refuses
to accept anything except cattle of a certain unusual colour. The
saint assembles the requisite number of cattle without regard to
their colour, and proceeds to change them to the colour Arthur
demands. When the latter comes to drive them away, they suddenly become bundles of bracken, and not until he has repented
of his obstinacy, begged the saint's forgiveness, and granted him
the right of giving sanctuary to fugitives, do the cattle regain
their normal form.

There is a hint of the influence of the later romances in the
first incident, especially in the idea of helping the distressed. The
second is typical of these stories, where a little pagan magic is
used to help the saint's reputation, and the principle that the
greater the rank of the sinner, the greater the glory of the saint,
is held unquestioningly. This is equally true of the *Life of St.
Carannog*,[11] where Arthur enlists the saint's aid to overcome a
serpent, and of the *Life of St. Efflam*, which is the only extant
Breton tale that antedates the age of the romances.*

The Life of St. Gildas, by another Llancarfan monk, Caradoc,
was written about 1130.[13] We have already spoken of its story of
the feud between Gildas and Arthur in the previous chapter, as a
possible explanation of Gildas's omission of Arthur from his *De
Excidio Britanniae*. In addition to this, there is another incident,

* The *Life of St. Goeznovius*, again Breton, is spuriously dated as
1019, but is really *c.* 1150.[12]

apparently imported from secular tradition,[14] and which is an early form of the story of Lancelot and Guinevere. It runs as follows:

'Gildas . . . went aboard the boat, and arrived at Glastonbury . . . where King Melwas ruled the Summer Country. He was received by the abbot of Glastonbury, and taught the brothers and some of the laity, sowing the seed of the divine doctrines. Here he wrote the histories of the kings of the Britons. Glastonbury is the Town of Glass . . . first named thus in the British tongue. It was besieged by an innumerable host led by Arthur the tyrant, because Guennuvar his wife, carried away and violated by the aforesaid evil King Melwas, had been brought here because it was an unassailable place, defended securely by reed-beds, river and marshes. The rebellious king (Arthur) had sought the queen all around for a year, and had finally heard of her hiding-place. Thence he gathered the entire army of Cornwall and Devon, and the two enemies prepared for war. Seeing this, the abbot of Glastonbury, accompanied by the clergy and Gildas Sapiens, went into the midst of the battle-array and advised Melwas to make peace and return the queen. Thus she was returned in peace and goodwill, as was fitting.'

The influence of Gildas's own *De Excidio Britanniae* is evident here. Arthur, although he was not one of the tyrants against whom Gildas ranted in vain, is grouped among the wicked princelings of the period. The epithet 'rebellious', however, implies not political but spiritual rebellion, for he had earlier refused to obey Gildas, at least, according to the latter's biographer.

This is all the actual legendary and literary material about Arthur that we possess dating from the period between his lifetime and his appearance as a fully-developed figure of romance. Several writers refer to such traditions, but this is often in connection with the 'Breton hope', that Arthur would one day

return as 'a political saviour'. Leaving these aside for later discussion, only four writers remain. Hermann of Laon, writing of
a Breton visit to England in 1113,[15] tells us that while in Devon
the monks were shown 'the Chair and Oven of that king Arthur
famous in the stories of the Britons', and were told 'that that
same region had once been Arthur's'. William of Malmesbury,
in the original version of his *Gesta Regum Britanniae* (1125) says:
'This is that Arthur of whom the British tales rave today, who
plainly deserves not lying fables, but true stories . . .' Geoffrey
of Monmouth himself, whose account of Arthur is the basis of
much of the medieval development of his legend, says in the
preface to the *Historia Regum Britanniae*[16] that stories about
Arthur were nowhere recorded in writing, although known and
well remembered by many peoples, as if they were written down.
The monk Ailred of Rievaulx, in his *Speculum Caritatis*, tells
how a novice at his monastery (in north-east Yorkshire) was
never moved by pious stories, although he had wept over tales
which the people recited 'about some Arthur (Arcturus) or
other' before he had entered the monastery. Nor could this
refer to the *Historia Regum Britanniae*, for Ailred wrote in 1140,
and historians of the time accepted it as accurate; hence 'fables'
could not be applied to it, but might well describe the work of
some wandering story-teller.

From literature, or rather literary fragments we must turn for
a moment to art; and from England we must move to Italy. The
connection will not at first be obvious; for the work in question
is by no means well known. It is a carving on the north doorway,
or 'Porta della Pescheria', of Modena Cathedral, a semicircular
frieze on the archivolt. It represents what is generally agreed to
be an episode from Arthurian romance.[17] Reading from left to
right, we have the following figures, identified by carved labels
above them. First, an unnamed knight on horseback, fully
armed, follows Isdernus, bareheaded but mounted and equipped
with spear and shield. He is preceded by Artus de Bretania,
armed and mounted, who is attacking Burmaltus, who is on

foot and wields a hammer, but wears no mail. A barbican and moated castle at the top of the arch contain a woman, Winlogee, who is accompanied by an unarmed man, Mardoc. To the right of this, an armed knight, Carrado, rides out to attack Galvagin. There follow Galvariun and Che, with their lances on their shoulders. All the last three are armed and mounted; Artus, Galvariun and Che have banrerets on the ends of their lances.

Neither names nor situation will be familiar: but if we alter them to familiar forms, they become recognizable. A castle is being besieged by Arthur (Artus) Ider (Isdernus), a knight who appears in Welsh stories, Gawain (Galvagin), Arthur's nephew, Galvariun, and Kay (Che). The defenders are Durmart (Burmaltus), Caradoc (Carrado) and presumably Marrok (Mardoc), all of whom figure in the later Arthurian stories. The woman is Guinevere, Winlogee being a form of her Breton name. The situation is found in *Durmart le Gallois*, a French romance of *c.* 1230; but its original is the incident from the life of Gildas we have quoted earlier.

So far there is nothing remarkable in the carving; a not unfamiliar Arthurian scene, albeit rather far afield. But when it comes to the date of the work, much has to be explained. For although art historians cannot give precise dates on the basis of style alone, it is generally agreed that this sculpture was executed between 1100 and 1120, *before any Arthurian romances of any sort other than the fragments in Welsh had been written down.* This dating is confirmed by the record of the building of the cathedral[18] which tells us that a considerable part of the cathedral had been built and sculptures placed in position by 1106. This probably included the west front, which was one of the first parts of a Romanesque cathedral to be built. This west front has on it carvings which are so similar in style to those on the north door that they cannot be more than a decade earlier or later. Hence the latest date for the latter is 1116, more than twenty years before the earliest of the written romances.[19]

However incredible this sculpture may be, and however difficult to accept, we must explain how it came to be produced in
Italy at a time when we have no recorded legends of any substance about Arthur on his native soil. Such slender evidence as
we have already considered shows that some sort of legend about
Arthur was current among popular story-tellers of Wales, Cornwall and Brittany; in fact, among the Celtic races descended
from the Britons of Arthur's day. And when the continental
romances of two or three decades later are examined, they are
full of Celtic names and incidents. We can find parallels to some
of these names and incidents in Welsh stories; but often there
are bewildering and quite inexplicable discrepancies in an otherwise recognizably Welsh tale. Many hypotheses have been put
forward to cover these facts and weld them into a rational whole,
and long and complex arguments brought forward. We can only
summarize and give as clear an outline as possible.

Only one factor will reconcile the three points: Celtic tales,
French romances, and Italian sculpture. The Bretons came of
Celtic stock, had many points of contact with France, and, we
know from records, travelled widely throughout Europe. They
are the only link between Wales and France at this time, and it
seems that it must have been they who transmitted the tales.
This would explain the strange discrepancies between the
Welsh originals and the French versions. But there remains one
major obstacle: there is hardly any written trace of any Breton
version of these legends.

This need not deter us; for most of the Welsh legends were
only recorded in the memory of the bards, and told or sung at
feasts. Similarly, the Bretons must have had their bards; their
material may well have been the same as the Welsh, but they
were free to wander beyond their own borders into France in
search of an audience. Their stories would have attracted the
writers and poets of the newly-developed French vernacular,
and in much elaborated forms passed into literature proper.

Such, drastically compressed, is the core of the argument in favour of the Breton origin of the French romances. Many minor points support it; Bretons are recorded both in Yorkshire, near the monastery where Ailred of Rievaulx wrote of the 'fables about Arthur' in 1140, and in northern Italy, on their way to the First Crusade[20] in 1096, near Modena, where the carving on the cathedral was made a decade later. The names in the French romances often show traces of a double recension, and are closer to Breton than Welsh: Owein ap Urien of the triads appears as Yvain in French and Ivan in Breton, to name but one of many such examples. The Bretons would be more likely to know the taste of the French, and adapt the stories accordingly, whereas the Welsh, while knowing the stories better, would not be able to make them really popular. Nor were the Bretons by any means an uncultured race; among other talented men of the period of Breton stock we find Peter Abelard and Bernard of Chartres.

Even if we have lost the vast majority of these legends about Arthur, we can piece together something of the process which swelled their bulk to the considerable body of tales that the Bretons must have handed on to the French. The early Welsh poets told tales about Arthur mainly consisting of heroic deeds by him and a few followers. As his status grew, some of the remnants, much corrupted, of Celtic pre-Christian mythology were attached to him, and the deeds proportionately exaggerated. The Bretons would have had their own additions to make when they adopted the stories, and their alterations to them when they took them into France would again have increased their number and size. Finally, the French themselves would have added to them both before and in the process of writing them down. So it is hardly surprising that Arthur enters literature with many of the stock episodes of mythology and folklore attached to him and his followers—seven centuries of story-telling rarely diminishes the length of traditions and tales.

Arthur's period of transition from reality to romance was a long and complex one. He was remembered as a hero by the

Welsh bards, who embroidered and added to his legends in their own skilful way, and from Wales the stories were taken to Brittany by fellow-Celts, where once again they were increased. About 1050–1100, they came into great popularity here, and were spread into France by jongleurs and minstrels who wandered from castle to castle reciting at feasts. At these recitals Arthur caught the imagination of the French poets, who wrote the recitals down for the first time, usually as poems of their own, and gave us the earliest version of the legend of Arthur we possess today.

THREE

ARTHUR THE EMPEROR

On reading the title of the next work in the sequence of Arthurian literature one might infer that we had to return once more to the serious historical side of Arthur's career. But the matter-of-fact title, *Historia Regum Britanniae*,[1] of Geoffrey of Monmouth's work conceals one of the greatest fictitious stories in English literature, one which was to have much influence with succeeding generations, and which encouraged the development of a written legend in no small degree.

Only a few details of the life of its author are known. Geoffrey of Monmouth, or Geoffrey Arthur as he is sometimes called, was born about 1100, either of Welsh or Breton descent.[2] We first hear of him as a witness to charters in or near Oxford from 1129 onwards. He seems to have lived in Oxford, and to have been associated with Robert of Chesney, later Bishop of Lincoln, to whom he dedicated his last work, the *Vita Merlini*, and with Walter, archdeacon of Oxford, who is said to have provided him with the source of the *Historia*.[3] The link between the three men seems to have been the college of secular canons, St. George's, in Oxford, Walter being its provost and Robert one of the six canons. Although Oxford was not yet an established university, Geoffrey, who on two occasions calls himself 'magister', may have had some sort of teaching appointment.

His earliest surviving literary effort is the *Prophetiae Merlini*

25

(Prophecies of Merlin), which was later incorporated in the *Historia Regum Britanniae* as Book VII, and was completed about 1132–5. He tells us at the beginning of this book,[4] that he began the *Historia* first, intending to deal with the sayings of Merlin later. But stories about Merlin began to circulate from other sources, and he was urged by Alexander, Bishop of Lincoln, and others of his friends, to complete this book first. This he did; and the *Libellus Merlini* appeared independently before his major work. The *Historia Regum Britanniae* seems to have been started about 1130 and finished shortly after the death of Henry I in December 1135. From the dedications we learn that Geoffrey was seeking the patronage of some important figure to secure him an ecclesiastical appointment, but for the time being he was unsuccessful. It was not until after he had written the last of his three known works, the Latin poem *Vita Merlini*, in 1148, and dedicated it to the new bishop of Lincoln, Robert of Chesney, that he gained his object. Although he was ordained priest on February 11th, 1152, and before the end of the same month consecrated bishop of St. Asaph in Flintshire—probably through Robert's influence—the post was almost certainly a sinecure of the type held by professional writers like himself, and in any case Norman influence in the area was so unreliable that he may never even have visited his diocese. The legend according to which he was buried in the cathedral is certainly without foundation. He died three years after the appointment.

Geoffrey's main interest was not the Church; he entered it merely because it was the most convenient career for a literary man. We have no evidence in his writings of a religious bent; but in the times and circumstances this is by no means unusual. The greatest of the translators of the *Historia*, Maistre Wace, was given a canonry at Bayeux in similar fashion as a token of royal favour and in return for a commissioned work. Otherwise there is little more to be said of the man; it is his works in which we are really interested.

Before examining his two works on Merlin, something about

this strange figure must be said. Welsh literature before 1100 is by no means lacking in material about him. Geoffrey himself tells us that the prophecies are translations from the Welsh, and this is probably true. Even his most hostile critic, William of Newburgh, can find no more scathing remark than that he added much.[5] Some of the story of Merlin comes from Nennius's account of the boy Ambrosius,[6] whose history and prophecies are very similar in outline to those of Geoffrey's seer. Giraldus Cambrensis, writing at the beginning of the thirteenth century, carefully distinguishes between this Merlin, Merlin Ambrosius, and another Merlin, Merlin Sylvester,[7] and this remark leads us to Geoffrey's real source for Merlin, the prophet Myrrdin who figures in some more than usually obscure Welsh poems.[8] From the fragments of his story contained in them, we learn that the central characters were Myrddin himself, Gwenddolau, Gwendydd, and Rhydderch. In the battle of Arfderydd—probably Arthuret, near Carlisle—Rhydderch seems to have killed Myrddin's lord, Gwenddolau. This, and a vision in the sky during the battle, caused Myrddin to go mad. Gwendydd was his sister, but seems to have had some special part in the disaster which we know nothing about. In Geoffrey's *Vita Merlini* we meet all four again. Ganieda (Gwendydd) is in addition the wife of Rodarchus (Rhydderch), a detail which probably came from the lost part of the Welsh story.

Another source for these works comes from Scotland. Myrddin is identical with the Lailoken of certain Scottish legends preserved in the *Life of St. Kentigern*. Both have connections with Rhydderch, and the Welshman is called 'llallogan' at one point, obviously a parallel to the name Lailoken. From the latter comes Merlin's association with the forest of Celidon, as a result of which Merlin Sylvester is sometimes known as Merlin Celidonus.

These legends will recur in discussion of the romances; but Geoffrey only used them in his last work, for the *Prophetiae Merlini* as their title implies, have little to do with the biography of

Merlin, and are in any case based mainly on the utterances of Ambrosius, although some remarks may come from other Welsh and Scottish tradition. The result falls into three parts: prophecies concerning a period in the past for Geoffrey; those concerning the near future for Geoffrey; and a series of apocalyptic scenes. The first part, which would of course be the future for Merlin, is known as *ex post facto* prophecy; the predictions are composed after the event and attributed to someone who is supposed to have lived before it. Hence the references are clear in many instances, in spite of their cryptic form. The sinking of the White Ship in 1120 is alluded to as follows: 'The Lion's Cubs shall be transformed into fishes of the sea.' Henry I is of course the lion: his 'cubs' included the heir, Prince William, his only son, who was drowned in this disaster. This type of prophecy established (apparently) Merlin's reputation for accuracy in prediction, and Geoffrey goes on to make a number of vague allusions of great ambiguity in the second part. Occasionally he refers to projected schemes which have not yet come to fruition. These sketches of the future become more and more vague until they merge into the third section, the apocalypse, for which Geoffrey used the Bible and possibly classical sources, for suitable imagery.

As they are placed in the *Historia*, these prophecies point forward to its climax in Arthur's reign, and form an integral part of the structure: but they are often found separately, and enjoyed a wide independent popularity. Commentaries were numerous; the most elaborate is that once ascribed to Alanus de Insulis, probably in fact by Alan of Tewkesbury, written between 1167–1174. Many imitations of the *Prophetiae* itself followed, in almost every western European language, until Merlin was recognized from Iceland to Sicily as a prophetic figure of the greatest importance.

But it was not the *Prophetiae* alone that made Geoffrey's reputation; it was chiefly the work of which they usually form part, the *Historia Regum Britanniae* (*History of the Kings of Britain*). This is dated at 1135–6. The opening dedication shows clearly that Geoffrey was seeking favour with prominent men, for there are three versions of it, each corresponding to a change in the political situation. The earliest of these is that which names Robert of Gloucester alone. Robert had supported Matilda immediately after the death of Henry I, but when the crown went to Stephen, he swore allegiance to the latter. Geoffrey seems to have been inspired by this new political development to add the name of Stephen's chief supporter, Waleran de Beaumont, who had often been connected with Robert in earlier years. When Robert was on more intimate terms with the king, Geoffrey moved him into second place, and put Stephen at the head with the attributes formerly given to Robert, and omitted Waleran. This combination of Stephen and Robert could not have been later than April 1138, for in that month, Robert reverted finally to his former allegiance to Matilda. It is possible that Geoffrey then used the single dedication to Robert once again, for we should expect to find one to Stephen alone if Geoffrey had abandoned Robert's side.[9] This is the most obvious of Geoffrey's attempts to ingratiate himself with the ruling classes; but we shall find other, more subtle means used in the actual historical part of the work.

There are about two hundred manuscripts of the *Historia*, an enormous number for any medieval work. Most of them show only minor departures from the original text, but we have four which present a completely variant version. The dedication is omitted from all of them, and passages which Geoffrey has borrowed from elsewhere and then rephrased are quoted in the original form. Professor Hammer, who edited these manuscripts, regarded it as a late recension by some other writer, and considered the differences too great to regard both the so-called Vulgate and Variant versions as being Geoffrey's work. But it has since been suggested that this is in fact his early draft, which would seem *prima facie* more likely; and that some alterations to this draft have been made by another later hand.[10]

What were Geoffrey's sources? How historically reliable is his narrative? And what was the 'very ancient book in the British tongue' which he claims to have used? All three questions can best be answered by a study of the last point. In the dedication Geoffrey states clearly that he used such a book, which related the histories of all the British kings, from Brutus to Cadwallader, and that it was given to him by Walter, Archdeacon of Oxford. However, this book is now completely lost; we have nothing even remotely corresponding to it. But there is almost unanimous agreement among scholars that it never existed in the first place, at least, not in the form indicated by Geoffrey.[11] The invocation of a lost source to give authority to a fictitious work is by no means unusual in medieval literature; for example, the group of romances about Troy were based on an imaginary work by one Dares, which had a considerable history attached to its discovery, and several of the saints' lives mentioned in our last chapter use this same device. And Geoffrey's *Historia* is of much the same nature as the last—romantic rather than factual history; we need not therefore accuse him of actual fraud. Let us say rather that here is an early example of a since popular literary formula, and that Geoffrey himself never expected great historical weight to be given to the result. We have no definite evidence of his intentions, and the nature of his other works would indicate a bent for the fictional rather than the historical. It was a slightly credulous generation, who of course had none of the historical evidence or critical method of today, and who perpetuated the error made by Henry of Huntingdon in regarding it as an essay in history with serious foundation. Nor was any sharp distinction made by most historical writers between fact and fancy; Geoffrey was merely less scrupulous than many of his contemporaries in making this division.

But this does not mean to say that he used no other source than his own imagination. Although he has in places concocted entire histories out of almost nothing, he restrained himself enough to give the result a quite false air of reality that made these stories generally accepted as accurate in outline if not in detail until the eighteenth century. Just as Arthur, as Geoffrey depicts him, is unhistorical, so is much of the rest. Brutus of Troy, the supposed founder of the British race and kingdom, Lud, from whom London was said to have got its name, King Lear, of Shakespearian fame, Caesar's three attempts to conquer Britain, and final success only through treachery on the part of a British noble—all these are the products of Geoffrey's brilliant imagination working on a name or an odd reminiscence. Against this, we find only occasional touches of history: Caractacus appears, though Boadicea is conspicuously absent; the appeal of the Britons to Aetius is historical fact, as are also some of the details after Arthur's time. For the period after the withdrawal of the Roman legions, Geoffrey draws on what was at the time accepted history, Nennius's *Historia Britonum*, and uses it up to the beginning of Arthur's career. Other details show that he knew a number of Welsh legends. For example, the name of Arthur's father, Uther, may be due to a misunderstanding of 'Arthur mab uthr', Arthur the terrible, as Arthur son of Uther. Arthur's weapons[12] are derived from various such Welsh stories: Caliburnus, his sword, better known as Excalibur, is identical with Caledfwlch in the Welsh,[13] his lance Ron the same as Rhongomyniad, both found as his weapons in *Kulhwch and Olwen*. The name of his shield arises out of a confusion with that of his ship. The ship Pridwen appears in the poem *The Spoils of Annwfn*; the shield in Geoffrey's account.

Such was the material Geoffrey turned to his own purposes when he wrote the *Historia*; but before we turn to these purposes, the outline of Arthur's career in it, about one-third of the whole work, must be briefly sketched. Merlin's prophecies precede it and point the way to it, for Arthur's reign is the climax of the *Historia*. It is with Merlin's help that Arthur is born. Uther falls violently in love with Igerna, wife of his enemy, Gorlois of Cornwall, and is magically transformed (by Merlin) into the latter's likeness. He enters the castle of Tintagel in Gorlois's absence, and begets Arthur of her. On his return, he learns that Gorlois has been killed a few hours earlier. He therefore marries

Igerna at the earliest opportunity, and Arthur thus enjoys the benefit of being miraculously and yet almost legitimately conceived. On his father's death, he succeeds to the throne, being then fifteen, and he is crowned by archbishop Dubricius. His first campaign is against the Saxons, who had caused his father's death by poisoning him. He defeats their leader, Colgrim, in a series of battles, based on the twelve described by Nennius. Arthur's chief allies are the Bretons, who play an important part throughout his reign, and whose leader, Hoel, is second only to Arthur himself.

Having defeated the Saxons with Hoel's assistance, he settles the internal affairs of his kingdom, and marries Guanhumara, daughter of a Cornish nobleman, who is of course the Gwenhyfar of the Welsh and the Guinevere of Malory. His ambitions now rise to an imperial plane, and without any apparent effort he proceeds to conquer, or receive homage from, large areas of northern Europe. Ireland is his first objective, and its conquest is swiftly followed by that of Iceland, Gothland, and the Orkneys. Norway is overcome and given to his brother-in-law; Dacia (Denmark), Aquitaine and Gaul have to be subjugated before his appetite is temporarily sated.

He then returns to Britain to hold his Whitsuntide crownwearing; and it is here that Geoffrey waxes most eloquent over the glories of the court. However, immediately the festivities are concluded, there arrive messengers from Lucius Tiberius, the Roman emperor, demanding tribute on the grounds that Britain was once a Roman province. Arthur convenes a council of kings, who unanimously agree that the only possible answer to so outrageous a demand is to march on Rome at once.

The kingdom is entrusted to Mordred and the army prepares to embark at Hamo's Port (Southampton). On the night before departure, Arthur has a foreboding dream which presages the coming struggle between himself and Lucius, or, according to another interpretation, between himself and a giant. He proceeds to France, landing at Barfleur, where he hears that a giant has carried off and killed Hoel's niece. He therefore makes a detour to Mont Saint Michel, and disposes of the monster. Continuing his march to Burgundy, he hears that the Romans are encamped hard by. He sets off in pursuit, and, after various skirmishes,

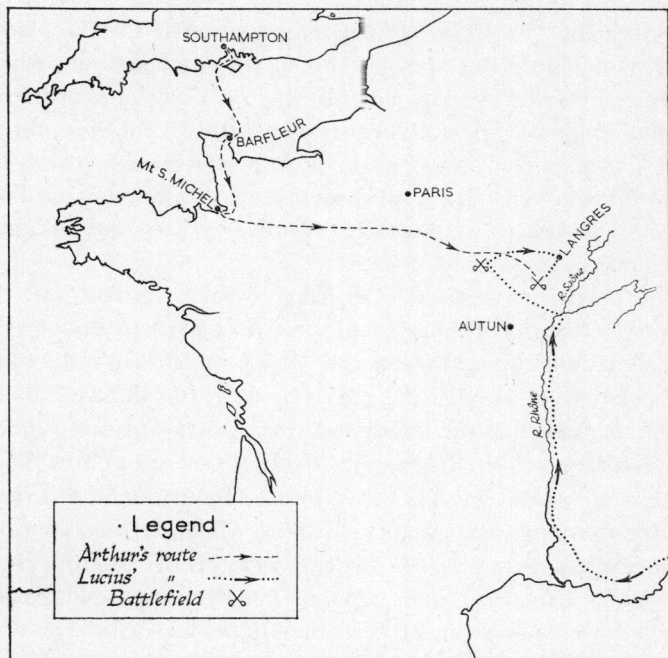

ARTHUR'S FRENCH CAMPAIGN

engages the main body of the army in a wooded valley near Langres. Lucius is killed and the Romans defeated, though not without considerable losses on the British side; notable among the slain are Kay and Bedivere.

Having thus cleared the way to Rome, Arthur is preparing to march south again, when he hears that Mordred has proved treacherous. He has usurped the crown and is about to marry Guinevere, having falsely spread the news that Arthur is dead.

D

On this Arthur immediately returns to Britain, dispatching the bodies of Lucius and various senators to Rome in lieu of the tribute.

At this point, Geoffrey begins a new book,[14] changes his style, and deals with the remainder of Arthur's reign in one-tenth of the space allotted to the Roman campaign. When Arthur lands in Britain, Mordred retires with his forces into Cornwall, where Arthur meets and engages him. In this final battle, Mordred is killed with almost all his followers; but Arthur's forces suffer no less, Arthur himself being taken to the mysterious Avalon for his wounds to be healed. Guinevere retires to a convent, and the kingdom passes to Constantine. Geoffrey's narrative becomes terse and seemingly historical.

The borderline between Geoffrey's own invention and the legendary material he has incorporated is hard to define. We have already compared the degree of historical fact and looked at the sources of some of the names he uses; but these are by no means so elusive as the incidental stories. The main outline of Arthur's career in the *Historia* is Geoffrey's own; but how much of the detail came from his fertile brain? One incident, a curious chapter on marvellous ponds in Britain, which Arthur describes to Hoel at the end of the Saxon campaign,[15] is drawn from Nennius's *Mirabilia*, and is incorporated for no apparent reason. Similarly the episode on Mont Saint Michel has little to do with the main military campaign; both this and another giant-killing recounted by Arthur afterwards come from a totally different atmosphere of personal strength and valour, and are found independent of Arthur himself in later Welsh legend.[16] Geoffrey probably used both incidents to increase Arthur's personal stature, but has failed to harmonize them with the rest of his narrative.

But Geoffrey has done a great deal more than simply combine the Welsh legendary and historical portraits of Arthur. He has formed an entirely new portrait as a result of his alterations to the plot; and a study of these changes will show us what he intended the new Arthur to represent, as well as revealing some of his other motives in writing the *Historia*.

We have already quoted Nennius's remark about Arthur that 'though there were many more noble than he, yet was he twelve times chosen commander', and suggested that here was a possible reason for the later elaboration of Arthur's birth. Geoffrey may have remembered this; but he was also thinking of the two chief figures in contemporary romances, Charlemagne and Alexander. It is the latter's biography that seems to have supplied the idea of a magical birth involving disguises and transformations.[17] Alexander's father in these stories was not Philip, his mother's husband, but one Nectanebus, a wizard and exiled king of Egypt, who arrived in Macedonia during Philip's absence and fell in love with his wife Olympiades. He told her that the god Ammon would come to her in the shape of a dragon which would then turn into a man; and a great hero would be born to her. However, Philip returns unexpectedly, but consents to receive the strange visitor and then retire. It is in fact Nectanebus himself who arrives under this disguise, and in due course Alexander is born. Both these stories may come from that of Jupiter and Amphitryon, which is in many ways a closer parallel to that of Uther and Igerna. The general idea of some mystery attached to the birth of a great hero is present in all three, and Geoffrey uses the story to raise Arthur to the status of Alexander and Hercules.

The other striking development is that of Arthur's continental and Scandinavian empire.[18] This is not difficult to trace. At the time Geoffrey was writing, just before the death of Henry I, the rulers of Britain were beginning to think once more in terms of overseas dominions of which Britain would be the centre. Geoffrey, by taking an earlier empire of which Britain had been the centre, and combining it with that of Charlemagne, the other great contemporary hero of romance besides Alexander, was merely catering for current taste and interest. The first empire was that of Canute, who would have represented to Geoffrey

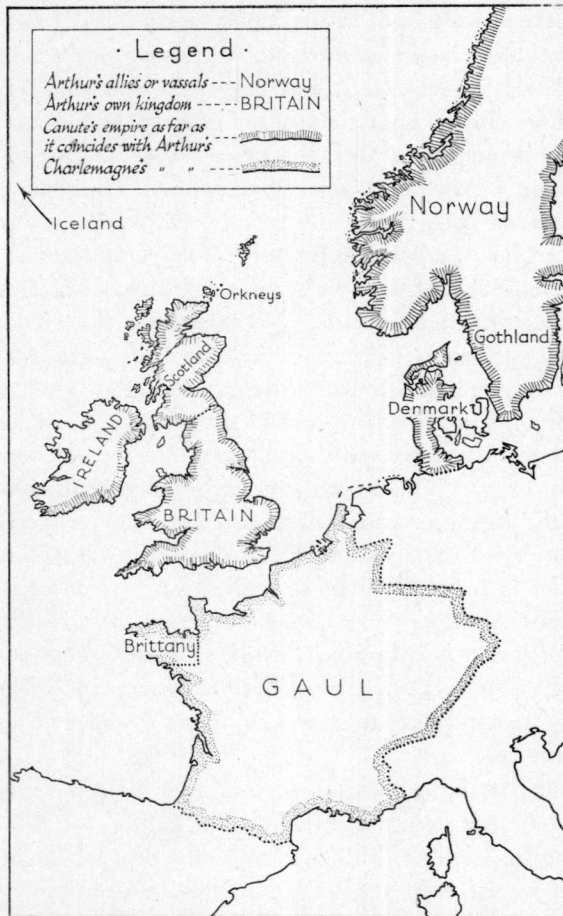

· Legend ·

Arthur's allies or vassals --- Norway
Arthur's own kingdom ----- BRITAIN
Canute's empire as far as
it coincides with Arthur's   ------
Charlemagne's   "   "   ------

Iceland

Norway

Orkneys

Gothland

Scotland

Denmark

IRELAND

BRITAIN

Brittany

GAUL

THE EXTENT OF ARTHUR'S EMPIRE ACCORDING TO
GEOFFREY OF MONMOUTH, AND ITS RELATION TO
THOSE OF CANUTE AND CHARLEMAGNE

· Legend ·

Arthur's route   — — — — — — — —
                    ⎰ 1067-8 ·····
William's routes   ⎱ 1068   · — · → · —
                    ⎱ 1069   · — · · → · ·
Area of campaign in Northumberland × × × ×
   "   "   "   " Cornwall ∘∘∘∘∘∘∘∘∘∘
Sites of Arthur's battles in Nennius ⚔

THE ENGLISH CAMPAIGNS OF WILLIAM AND ARTHUR

Arthur set out from Silchester, relieved York, and Lincoln, went north to Dumbarton, then south to relieve Bath, returned to Dumbarton to defeat the Picts in Galloway, and ended in York.

William set out from London, fought a campaign in the South-West, followed by the 'harrying of the North' and the overthrow of Hereward the Wake in the Fens, and ended in York.

what Napoleon I would to a Frenchman of today; he had ruled all the lands in Arthur's empire except for those in France, which were Charlemagne's, and Ireland, over which he had, however, claimed suzerainty.

Arthur's campaigns against the Saxons are described at great length. Parallels can be drawn between the English campaigns of William I and those of Arthur. But the main source of inspiration seems to have remained Nennius, from whom eight of the battles are adopted directly, albeit under Geoffrey's interpretation of their sites, which was evidently a matter of doubt in his day. None the less, the events immediately following the campaigns offer a remarkable resemblance. In 1069 William spent Christmas at York, which had been laid waste by Normans and Danes in turn. He appointed a new archbishop, the former prelate having recently died, and drew up plans for the general restoration of the city. When compared with Arthur's actions the connection cannot be lightly set aside.[19] Arthur is specifically stated to have been at York for Christmas, and he similarly appoints a new archbishop, although William does not seem to have appointed his personal chaplain, as Arthur did. There can be no doubt as to the link; but the campaigns that precede have little in common, and the stay at York marked the end of Arthur's campaigns, whereas William had yet to subdue the Fens.

On considering these sources of inspiration, we begin to get an idea of Geoffrey's object in writing the *Historia*. He seems to be attempting to provide the Britons with an emperor-hero to whose golden age they could look back with pride. France had Charlemagne; the Greeks, Alexander; and the Saxons, Beowulf and kindred heroes. Arthur's history is modelled, as has been shown, on the first two; but Geoffrey is no slavish imitator. It is the concept of the emperor-hero that he has adopted, rather than minor details. In fact, he succeeds in incorporating much national material in the execution of this idea, and gives it a suitably British outlook. All these imperial chronicles lie on the borderline of history and romance, and Geoffrey is merely more obviously inclined to fiction than the others. It is a conscious attempt to create a national epic, in the same way as the *Aeneid*, or, a closer parallel, the *Franciad* of Pierre de Ronsard.

Geoffrey's other object is to provide politically useful precedents. Even if his work as a whole is unhistorical, there is enough accurate material in it to make fact and fiction hard to distinguish, as we have seen. So his work could be quoted with reasonable safety in cases where a precedent was required. Brittany and Scotland are two examples of this. The Bretons play a considerable part in the *Historia*, but are rarely found in connection with Arthur elsewhere. If we look at the contemporary political situation of Brittany and England, we shall find a possible reason for this bias on Geoffrey's part. A tenuous claim to overlordship of Brittany had been advanced by the Normans since the days of William the Conqueror, and this was only confirmed in 1113. The Duchy of Brittany was, however, still poised between independence and the feudal suzerainty of Britain, and in any case was a valuable ally. So a reminder of the connection between the two countries was likely to go down well with the Norman court, and a little flattery of the Bretons would be regarded favourably. As for Scotland, Edward III in a letter to the Pope of 1301, actually quotes the *Historia* in support of his claim to it. Geoffrey, albeit rather belatedly, seems to have been successful in his object.

The question of the large role assigned to the Bretons in the *Historia* is interesting, for they vanish completely from Arthurian romance except in those works directly based on Geoffrey. He seems to have had some special, possibly personal, reason for giving them this part. The idea of creating a precedent has already been mentioned. It has also been suggested that he was of Breton, not Welsh blood, and his sympathies would seem to be inclined to the Bretons at the expense of the Welsh. The latter are by no means idealized in the more recent part of the *Historia*; but it is possible that many of his hostile remarks come from

Gildas's *De Excidio Britanniae*. Finally, it is conceivable that the 'very ancient book' which he quotes as the source for the *Historia*, although probably fictitious, may have been a volume of British genealogies from Brittany, and hence with a Breton bias.

The main framework of Geoffrey's book is fictitious, and partly written with an eye to contemporary politics. But this framework is filled out with considerable details of life in the days of which he speaks. These must also be imaginary; but we should hardly expect any attempt on Geoffrey's part at historical realism. The descriptions of the sixth-century court are drawn entirely from contemporary life. On every page we find customs or manners that would have been entirely out of place in the historical sixth century, but are entirely in harmony with what is known of those of the twelfth. As far as Arthur's court is concerned, the most important passage is that describing his crown-wearing at the City of Legions immediately after his campaigns in Gaul against the Romans.[20] The City is here described at length; its churches of St. Julius and St. Aaron, its convent of canons and college of philosophers, until the magnificence of the court itself makes even the loquacious Geoffrey pause for words. He can hardly be thinking of the English court of the twelfth century in all this splendour; and a few lines further on, he relates a custom which at once betrays the place that inspired this description. When it comes to the church ceremony, the women go to a separate church; afterwards they hold their own banquet, at the same time as that of the men. These manners have a strong Eastern flavour; and the only place where they were combined with Christianity was at Constantinople, a favourite stopping-place for the returning Crusader. It was regarded as the most luxurious city in the world, and it is obviously the model for Geoffrey's City of Legions. Once again, Arthur has risen at one step to the heights of glory from a not very distinguished position.

For one of the earliest writers of fiction in the Middle Ages, Geoffrey succeeds remarkably well. But in one thing his touch is not so sure. The methods of warfare throughout the *Historia* are strangely inconsistent; they correspond with no known tactics or equipment, and yet occasionally the latest developments of Geoffrey's day appear. He seems to have relied on very indirect reports which he cannot really have understood.[21]

The *Historia Regum Britanniae* is the greatest single contribution to Arthurian romance: it provided the entire historical part of them, which appears chiefly in the Merlin branch of the romance cycles, and was more extensively known and used by later writers than any other part of the legend. It is a plausible account, and in this lies Geoffrey's greatest achievement. He produced an historical romance, which, whether he intended it or not, was lifelike enough for his successors to be taken for history for six hundred years after his death, and up to the beginning of the nineteenth century it was on Geoffrey of Monmouth's story rather than on Malory's that the English conception of Arthur was founded.

As an author, Geoffrey had an immediate success by medieval standards. Since the spread of written works depended on laborious hand-copying of manuscripts, reputations in the literary field were slow in the making, but the *Historia* was accepted and enthusiastically read by most historians of the time, and there was very little opposition to it. William of Newburgh is the first writer to object to it in strong terms, at the end of the twelfth century. In the introduction to his *Historia Rerum Anglicarum*,[22] he attacks Geoffrey's excessive praise of the British race, his stories about Arthur and Merlin, which had of course been Geoffrey's own largest contribution to the work, and his acceptance of the Bretons' hope of the return of Arthur, implied in the transference of Arthur to Avalon, and developed in the later *Vita Merlini*. Giraldus Cambrensis, while often citing it as though historical, also tells a story of a man plagued by evil spirits, by which he was able to pick out false passages in books. When St. John's Gospel was placed on his breast, the spirits vanished; but when, by way of experiment, it was replaced by 'Geoffrey

Arthur's book', they returned, more horrible and numerous than ever before. He thus implies that he realized the true nature of the work.

But most chroniclers and historical writers followed the *Historia* without question. Henry of Huntingdon, in a letter to a certain Warinus in 1139, gives a summary of it to supplement his own Saxon history, and declares his astonishment at finding the work, which he was shown at Bec, on his way home from Rome. Alfred of Beverley, about 1150, was the first to incorporate it into the standard form of historical work of the period, the monastic chronicle, although he does question some parts and reject others. Some fifty other Latin chroniclers up to 1420 used it to a greater or lesser extent, and it was recognized as the standard work on the period.

Nor were the poets slow to adopt it. Within two decades, two translations of Geoffrey had appeared in French, and within half a century a Middle English version, taken from the French, followed, in addition to the numerous chronicle abridgements. We no longer possess the first of the French versions, by one Geoffrey Gaimar, but we know something of it from his other work, *Lestorie des Engles* (*The History of the English*) which forms a sequel to it. As far as we can tell, it must have been completed within a decade or so of the original, *c.* 1145–50.[23]

It was however rapidly superseded by Maistre Wace's *Roman de Brut*, probably a much superior work from the literary point of view. Wace was born in Jersey about 1100, and in his youth lived at Caen, where he studied for some time, completing his education in the Ile de France. On his return to Caen, he wrote his first 'romanz', or tales in verse, which included some saints' lives. Before writing the *Roman de Brut*, he seems to have visited southern England, possibly through a connection between the two great Caen monasteries and Dorset. In 1155, just twenty years after the *Historia Regum Britanniae*, he completed his version of it;[24] we learn from his English translator, Layamon, that a copy was given to Queen Eleanor,[25] whose husband, Henry II, had ascended the throne in the previous year. Wace soon received a commission from the king to write a history of the dukes of Normandy, and he started this, the *Roman de Rou*, in 1160. In 1169, he was appointed to the canonry of Bayeux as a token of royal favour, but since he had still not finished the commissioned work in 1174, Henry asked another poet, Maistre Beneeit, to finish it. He must have died shortly after 1175, when his name is found for the last time.

The *Roman de Brut*, so named after Brutus, whom Geoffrey of Monmouth made the founder of Britain,* is largely based on the *Historia Regum Britanniae* in both Vulgate and Variant versions. Much of the apparent expansion (from 6,000 lines of Latin prose[26] to 15,000 of French verse) is due to the shortness of the verse line. But Wace has treated his material with some freedom, like most medieval translators. His personal knowledge of southern England caused some alterations, especially in the account of the campaign against the Saxons. The oral tradition must have supplied him with the element of courtly love, which is absent from Geoffrey, and there is a definitely romantic tone to the whole work, which contrasts with Geoffrey's drier, more historical phrases. Versification heightens this linguistic difference, and many similes are added. Direct speech is much more extensively used, and the writer's attitude is, as might be expected, emotional rather than detached; both factors increase the vividness of the narrative considerably. The sea and nautical affairs, scarcely noticeable in Geoffrey, are much to the fore in the *Brut*, possibly because of Wace's childhood environment in Jersey. Lastly and somewhat surprisingly, there is a rational and sceptical approach, as a result of which Merlin's role is minimized and the Prophecies entirely omitted on the grounds that they are unintelligible.

The main outline, however, remains similar. Wace seems

* This practice of inventing founders of countries by using a character in classical legend with a similar name was common in medieval times. Cf. *Sir Gawain and the Green Knight*, stanza 1, where four instances occur.

either to have been ignorant of Gaimar's earlier French version, or intentionally ignored him, for there are fewer alterations than would be compatible with such a double rewriting of Geoffrey. The section concerning Arthur has only one major addition. He relates that Arthur, because his barons could not agree on an order of precedence in seating 'made the Round Table, of which the Bretons tell many a tale'. It is probable, although still disputed, that the Round Table does in fact come from Celtic tradition, and the Bretons may well have been Wace's immediate source.[27] Most of Wace's other additions come from classical legend or local tradition, and this highly unusual idea is not in keeping with his normal level of invention. However, the passage in Wace has little interest *per se*; it is only later developments that lend it significance.

It was in Wace's work that Arthur himself reached his widest recognition as a poetical figure. Later works may be more popular, or magnify Arthur to a greater extent, but the two factors never coincide again as they do here. No less than twenty-four manuscripts of the *Roman de Brut* survive, and, even if this figure palls beside the mass of manuscripts of its original, it is more than any other medieval French work save one.* From it, all other subsequent chronicles of the legendary history of Britain were known as *Bruts*. Several of these fall within our scope.

The first of these is also the first English vernacular version of the Arthurian legend of which we have record. It is the *Brut* of Layamon,† who, as he himself tells us, was a parish priest of Areley Regis on the upper reaches of the Severn in Worcestershire. His name indicates Scandinavian origin, but it is unlikely that he was of Norse-Irish stock, as has been suggested.[28] He completed this, his only known work, between 1189–99.

It is a translation from Wace's French from beginning to end; in spite of an introductory statement that he had used Bede in an

* Benoit's *Roman de Troie* (39 MSS.).
† The Middle English spelling is Laʒamon; pronunciation would require a spelling of Lawman, but ʒ has become y or g in modern English, and hence spelling used.

English translation and 'the book of SS. Albin and Augustine'—
probably a Latin version of Bede—as well as the *Roman de Brut*.
Most of the additional material is his own: with this, the total
length of 32,000 lines is twice that of the previous version. Just
under one-third is concerned with Arthur.[29]

Once again the expansion of the story is in detail rather than in
the basic plot. Simile, rare in the Anglo-Saxon poets, is very
extensively used: a fine example is the description of dead knights
in the River Avon—'steel fishes lie in the stream . . . their scales
float like gold-painted shields, their fins float as if they were
spears'. Many set phrases are repeated whenever a set character
or situation reappears, which swells the text considerably. His
vocabulary is largely Saxon, with not more than 200 romance
words in the whole work, and a great variety of synonyms
inherited from the earlier poets.[30] As in Wace, details are
embroidered and elaborated,[31] and still more direct speeches
added.

The influence of chivalry is entirely lacking, and in fact Layamon's alterations tend to be in the other direction; the pendulum
has swung back to Geoffrey of Monmouth's sources as far as the
general atmosphere is concerned. He explains and simplifies
situations rather than complicating them, as would be only
natural for a writer whose audience was the common people
rather than the royal court. Although the French romances were
by now in full spate,* there is no trace of any of the later heroes,
and the native characters retain their original qualities: Kay is
still the brave and valiant knight of Welsh legend, and shares
with Bedivere many of the adventures, which are military rather
than knightly. Gawain is second only to the king, as in most
native English works, while Hoel's considerable part in the *Historia Regum Britanniae* has been drastically reduced. Merlin's
role has also become a minor one; he no longer dominates the
work in the same way when he appears. It is Arthur, and Arthur
alone, who has any real importance; his character here reaches

* See Chapter 5.

its zenith. He is neither the somewhat crude and vigorous leader of the Welsh tales, although it is to the barbaric rather than the aesthetic that his splendour inclines, nor the *roi fainéant* of lascivious tendencies found in the French romances. His courage, generosity, sincerity and leadership are all brought out: but they are seen through the eyes of a simpler culture, and are harmonized with the tone of the work as a whole. This is less refined and literary in style than its sources, as is to be expected, and the attitude of the poet is markedly less civilized. Thus Arthur, although he laments his fallen knights with great tenderness, is ferocious towards his enemies in a way that we cannot easily understand today. Yet this ferocity was commonplace in Layamon's time, and examples can be found everywhere in its popular tales and art. For instance, the doom paintings in almost every church in the country were scarcely less savage in spirit than Arthur's exultation over the dead Kolgrim, the Saxon leader: 'Even if you desired to go to heaven, you shall go to hell, ever to remain there, never to return.' None the less, barbaric though it is, Arthur's personal splendour remains impressive.

The account of the Round Table is an important expansion of Wace. Layamon tells us how, at a Christmas feast attended by seven kings' sons with 700 knights, a quarrel over precedence arose, and several men were killed in the ensuing fight. Peace was only restored with difficulty. When Arthur went to Cornwall shortly afterwards, he met a carpenter from foreign lands, who had heard about the incident and offered to make him a table which could be carried anywhere, and at which sixteen hundred men could sit without one being higher than the next. He was provided with materials and completed it in six weeks. The association with Cornwall, and the exaggerated and miraculous nature of the table, are probably remnants of the Celtic original, which may have been an Irish saga.[32]

One element that at first appears to be out of keeping with an heroic conception of Arthur is that of faery. Yet this is introduced by Layamon with some success. A natural part of many stories familiar to his audience, it adds an aura of dignified mystery; both at his birth and death, he is attended by supernatural beings—'elves' is scarcely the right word for the Saxon 'elven'. These, it is implied, give him their support throughout his life, and Argante,* their queen, carries him away at his death. The closing scene of Arthur's life in Layamon is only rivalled by that in Malory, and it is therefore worth quoting in full:

> ' "Constantine, I leave you my kingdom; guard my Britons, and see that they keep the laws that I have given them. I myself will go to Avalon, where Argante, queen of faery, has her dwelling. She will heal my wounds, for her draughts make men whole again. And then I will return to reign joyfully over my kingdom again." And as he spoke, a little boat came over the waves, in which sat two ladies, richly dressed; and they bore Arthur at once to the boat, and laid him gently down, and the boat sped away. But the British folk say that Arthur yet lives in Avalon, held by a magic spell, and they await his return.'

Layamon alters another supernatural event in Geoffrey's last chapter. This is Arthur's dream presaging the conflict between him and Lucius. In Layamon's version a different dream is described, and its import is different, for it foreshadows the treachery of Mordred and Guinevere. It is more dramatically conceived. Arthur is sitting on the roof of his hall with Gawain when Mordred appears with a throng of men, and starts to cut down the posts supporting the building. Guinevere aids him by tearing off the roof. The building collapses, killing Gawain, but Arthur escapes, and beheads Mordred and the Queen, to find himself alone on a wild moor. A golden lion approaches; he mounts it and is carried down to the sea-shore. The lion starts to swim out to sea with him, but he loses his grip on the lion's mane and is

---

* The initial letter M has probably been dropped: hence Morgan is the proper form.[33] She first appears in Geoffrey of Monmouth's *Vita Merlini* and is the same as Malory's Queen Morgan.

only rescued by a giant fish, which deposits him once again on the shore. Such symbolism, in this case reasonably straightforward, had great appeal for the medieval mind, as is shown by the popularity of the far less readily interpreted *Prophetiae Merlini*.

So it is in Layamon's *Brut* that Arthur reaches his personal zenith as a great emperor whose own deeds are the focal point of the story; and we might well expect it from a writer of Layamon's calibre. Geoffrey was an ambitious historian, Wace a courtly chronicler: both were trying to please and obtain the favour of the highest in the land. Layamon was a humble story-teller far more concerned with his actual tale, and much more forthright in his approval or disapproval of character, and lacked the subtle psychological analysis of the French writers,* as is shown by his handling of Guinevere; her transfer of affections to Mordred is abrupt, taking place only when the plot requires it. Hence, although the resulting work is one of the masterpieces of the time, it never gained the popularity of the other two, and its influence on later writers is negligible. We have only two manuscripts,[34] of which one is a slightly abbreviated form. So later chroniclers' accounts are drawn from Wace or Geoffrey rather than from Layamon. Of these, we need only discuss those which are exclusively Arthurian or of particular merit.

The first of these, known as the *Thornton*† or alliterative *Morte Arthure*, is a poem of considerable merit, 4,346 verses in length, composed between 1350–1400 in the North of England or south Scotland. It has been ascribed by some critics to Huchown of the Awle Ryale, on the authority of a passage in Andrew Wyntoun's *Chronykil of Scotland*, which states that among his works was a poem entitled *The Gret Geste of Arthure*.‡

* See Chapter 5.
† From the name of the copyist, Robert of Thornton, to distinguish it from the totally different stanzaic or Harleian *Le Mort Arthur*.
‡ Wyntoun, *Chronykil of Scotland*, ll.4329 ff. From what he tells us of it, it was an alliterative poem involving the emperor Lucius, who is Arthur's Roman opponent.

The identity of this with the *Morte Arthure* is still doubtful in the extreme. The poem has undergone much alteration during transcription, as can be seen by comparison with those parts of Malory based on another copy of it, and parts seem to have been written down from memory by the last copyist, to the disadvantage of the work as a whole.

Its basis appears to have been the *Historia Regum Britanniae*, with some additions from later works, including the version of Wace on which Layamon's *Brut* was based, the '*chansons de geste*', notably that of *Fierabras*, from which is drawn the encounter of Gawain and Priamus, and finally the romances of which Alexander is the hero. The vivid dramatization that has taken place, in a different idiom but on the same lines as that carried out by Wace and Layamon, requires no other source than the anonymous writer's own imagination. Many other departures from the original can be explained by what may be termed the contemporary reference process. Just as Geoffrey of Monmouth drew on events and politics of his own times, and thus created parallels between his portrait of Arthur and the Norman kings, so the author of the *Morte Arthure* has to some extent modelled Arthur and his deeds on the Plantagenets and their campaigns.[35] Nor was he the last to use this process, for in Malory's portrait of the same king are traces of Henry V.* A few instances from the poem may be used in illustration. The scene of the great battle against Lucius Tiberius exactly resembles that of Crecy. A sea-fight is introduced, which appears to be a description of that off Winchelsea against the Spanish fleet in 1350; the author mentions Spaniards where the sense would require Romans, and this may well be a slip of the pen. Mordred and Roger Mortimer have several points in common, and the charges brought against him are similar to those of Mortimer's impeachment. Hoel's niece, who in Geoffrey played a very minor role, becomes Duchess of Brittany and niece to Arthur, thus presenting an analogy with Jeanne de Montfort, who was similarly related to

* See chap. 7.

E

Edward III, and held the same title. Lorraine, where most of Arthur's battles are fought, is probably meant to be the Brittany of Edward III's campaigns in 1340–5. But Arthur's imperial ambitions cannot be paralleled in Edward's career, and the fact that Arthur is about to be crowned when he is forced to return,* is also an entirely novel idea.

Other additions are purely incidental, but none the less interesting. Arthur's route through Italy follows that given in the thirteenth-century itinerary by one Adam of Domerham in general outline, but mention of places not included in that work implies a more intimate knowledge of the country, either on the part of the writer himself or of one of his acquaintances. Few travellers other than diplomatic emissaries made the journey from England to Rome, but in 1350 a party of 400 pilgrims went there for the jubilee year celebrations. It is reasonable to assume that either the writer or his informant were among them, especially since the whole idea of Arthur's invasion of Italy is only found in this one work.

Before Arthur is forced to abandon his imperial pretensions, he has a dream in which he sees himself as one of the great emperors, bearing the symbols of imperial coronation, and seated on one of the nine chairs of Fortune's wheel. He reaches the highest point of the wheel, and, like his predecessors, is dashed down at the next turn of it. This symbol of earthly vanity and mortality is common in medieval literature, but good use of it is made here. Finally, on his return from the Continent, Arthur engages Mordred in a sea-fight on the beach, in which Gawain is killed. Both Arthur and Mordred speak movingly of his greatness. The final battle follows, and Arthur, although victorious as usual, is mortally wounded and buried at Glastonbury.

There is considerable literary merit in this poem. Characterization is good, and Mordred, usually a mere villain, has some dignity and is able to command our sympathy. He seems to have

* In Geoffrey of Monmouth's account he does not even cross the Alps into Italy.

forebodings of an inescapable tragedy, an idea which indeed per-
vades the work, and is typified by the 'Wheel of Fortune' dream;
for this reason he is reluctant to become regent in Arthur's
absence. Arthur's eulogy of Gawain is one of the finest pieces of
writing in the romances of this kind, most speeches on such
occasions being merely insipid. Gawain retains his character as
the flower of Arthur's knights, although the detracting influence of the French verse romances is elsewhere apparent,
and it is as his greatest warrior that Arthur praises him.

The setting of several early morning scenes, especially that at
Mont Saint Michel before Arthur's combat with the giant, show
a pleasant, if conventional, feeling for nature. His descriptions of
battle scenes are superb, the alliterative verse lending itself to
such passages admirably. As a whole the poem is one of the more
impressive English productions of the period, being neither too
close an imitation of the French, nor too crude a story, but with
its own special, aristocratic, appeal.

Only one other chronicle-poem is purely Arthurian. It is
attached to a Latin chronicle of the kings of Britain, and is
roughly contemporary with the *Morte Arthure*. It is 642 verses
long, in rhyming stanzas, the dialect being southern. The writer
seems to have thought it inappropriate to describe Arthur's
career in anything other than English, and the result is an
abbreviated 'historical' account, precisely and pedantically written, evidently with didactic object.

The later chroniclers and historians are of lesser importance.*[36]
Between 1150 and 1350 there were several poetic versions of
Geoffrey, notably those of Robert of Gloucester, Peter Langtoft,
and Robert Mannyng of Brunne, the latter being best known for
his translation of the *Manuel des Péchés*, *Handlyng Sinne*. He
also gives the best version of Arthur's history. When the first
Scottish chronicles appeared, they rapidly became hostile to
Arthur for nationalistic reasons, as in John of Fordun (*c.* 1385).
Hector Boece represents the climax of this movement in his

* See Chronological Tables.

Scotorum Historia of 1528, where Mordred appears as the right-ful heir, supplanted by Arthur, and the latter is portrayed in the worst possible light.

Some thirty years earlier, in England, Robert Fabyan, in his *New Chronicles* had cast serious doubt on Geoffrey's account for the first time in three centuries, and as a result he omitted the romantic and supernatural elements of the *Historia*. This atti-tude continued until Polydore Vergil, in his *Anglicae Historiae* of 1534 modified Geoffrey more than was felt right, and a moderate reaction took place. The *Historia Regum Britanniae* was defended by several later writers, but with the advent of real historical criticism in the seventeenth century, the obviously legendary parts were rejected. Yet it was not until the end of the eighteenth century that the whole outline was labelled as historically un-acceptable. It says much for the merits of the *Historia* that it was able to deceive historians for six hundred years into a totally false view of the period it covered. The romantic history of Geoffrey of Monmouth has permanently coloured the English idea of Arthur: its writer could not have hoped for greater success than this.

FOUR

ARTHUR AND AVALON

ARTHUR in the twelfth and thirteenth centuries was not only the central figure of a vast literature, a subject for poets and their patrons, but there had also grown up around him a widespread belief that he would one day return as the saviour of the British peoples, to lead them once more to their ancient supremacy over their island. As early as the seventh or eighth century, in a Welsh poem entitled *Verses on the Graves of the Heroes*, we find that he is regarded as something of an enigma in this respect: 'Concealed till Doomsday is the grave of Arthur.'*[1] More definite in content is the incident in a French work by one Hermann of Laon, concerning a visit to Britain by some French canons with a holy relic:

'From thence (Exeter) we went into the province called Devon, where they showed us the Chair and Oven of that king Arthur famous in the stories of the Britons, and they said that that same land had once been Arthur's. . . .

'In the town called Bodmin . . . a certain man with a withered hand kept watch in the presence of the relic in

* On this important point there is unfortunately wide variance as to translation. Another writer's version[2] reads: 'An eternal wonder is the grave of Arthur.' But the underlying implication is agreed to be that Arthur's death was mysterious, and the possibility of his return was hinted at.

53

order to be cured. But, just as the Bretons are wont to quarrel with the French about King Arthur, the same man began to argue with one of our monks, Haganellus, related to the archdeacon Guido of Laudun, saying that Arthur was still alive. No little tumult arose out of this; a crowd burst into the church carrying weapons, and had not Algardus, head of the clergy, interrupted, blood might well have been shed. Since we believed that the quarrel which had taken place in front of the relic displeased our Lord, the man with the withered hand did not recover his health.'[3]

This incident occurred in 1113, some twenty years before the first major Arthurian work was written down, and is valuable testimony to the currency of stories by word of mouth about Arthur. The fierceness with which this belief in his return was supported is also noteworthy; it argues a well-established tradition, and indeed within a few years this tradition seems to have assumed the proportions of a political force, invoked in Welsh rebellions against the English. We have other evidence of such stories around this period, notably that of William of Malmesbury. Speaking of the discovery of Gawain's grave some forty years earlier, he says: 'But the grave of Arthur is nowhere to be seen, whence ancient songs prophesy that he is yet to come.'[4]

Geoffrey of Monmouth, as one would expect, has heard of the tradition, and makes use of it, but with the introduction of a new element. Arthur is described as being borne away to Avalon. We learn from the *Vita Merlini* that this is a sort of 'other-world' Garden of the Hesperides, an Isle of Apples presided over by nine fays, of whom Morgan is the chief. The Avalon-Isle of Apples identification was to recur later; but let us follow the fortunes of the legend of Arthur's return until then.

Henry of Huntingdon, in his summary of Geoffrey in a letter to a certain Warinus in 1139, uses similar words to those of William of Malmesbury: '. . . he himself received so many wounds that he fell; although his kinsmen the Britons deny that he was

mortally wounded and seriously expect he will come again.'[5] An
independent witness is that of Alan of Tewkesbury in 1170, in
his commentary on Merlin's prophecies: 'And he continued:
His departure will be obscured by doubt, which is indeed true,
for there are today varying opinions as to his life and death. If
you do not believe me, go to the kingdom of Armorica, that is,
lesser Britain, and preach in the villages and market-places that
Arthur the Briton died as other men die; and then, if you escape
unharmed, for you will be either cursed or stoned by your
hearers, you will indeed discover that Merlin the prophet spoke
truly when he said that Arthur's departure would be obscured by
doubt.'[6] Other followers of Geoffrey echo these words in
variously embellished forms; the greatest version is probably
that of Layamon, which has already been quoted.

But Geoffrey himself, by mentioning Avalon as Arthur's
resting-place, whether from Welsh legend or by a new association of his own invention, had sowed the seeds of the eventual
obliteration of the so-called 'Breton hope'. For some fifty years
later, Avalon and Arthur were identified and his grave opened to
the world—or so the monks of Glastonbury claimed.

The fullest account of the discovery of this grave, which took
place in 1190 or 1191 is given by Giraldus Cambrensis two years
later, and is worth quoting in full:

'Arthur, the famous British king, is still remembered, nor
will this memory die out, for he is much praised in the history of the excellent monastery of Glastonbury, of which he
himself was in his time a distinguished patron and a generous
endower and supporter. . . . His body, for which popular
stories have invented a fantastic ending, saying that it had
been carried to a remote place, and was not subject to death,
was found in recent times at Glastonbury between two stone
pyramids standing in the burial ground. It was deep in the
earth, enclosed in a hollow oak, and the discovery was
accompanied by wonderful and almost miraculous signs. It

was reverently transferred to the church and placed in a marble tomb. And a leaden cross was found laid under a stone, not above, as is the custom today, but rather fastened on beneath it. We saw this, and traced the inscription which was not showing, but turned in towards the stone: "Here lies buried the famous king Arthur* with Guinevere† his second wife in the isle of Avalon."‡ In this there are several remarkable things: he had two wives, of which the last was buried at the same time as him, and indeed her bones were discovered with those of her husband; however, they were separate, since two parts of the coffin, at the head, were divided off, to contain the bones of a man, while the remaining third at the foot contained the bones of a woman set apart. There was also uncovered a golden tress of hair that had belonged to a beautiful woman, in its pristine condition and colour, which, when a certain monk eagerly snatched it up, suddenly dissolved into dust. Signs that the body had been buried here were found in the records of the place, in the letters inscribed on the pyramids, although these were almost obliterated by age, and in the visions and revelations seen by holy men and clerks; but chiefly through Henry II, King of England, who had heard from an aged British singer that his (Arthur's) body would be found at least sixteen feet deep in the earth, not in a stone tomb, but in a hollow oak. This Henry had told the monks; and the body was at the depth stated and almost concealed, lest, in the event of the Saxons occupying the island, against whom he had fought with so much energy in his lifetime, it should be brought to light; and for that reason, the inscription on the cross which would have revealed the truth, was turned inwards to the stone, to conceal at that time what the coffin contained, and yet inform other centuries. What is now called Glastonbury was in former times called the Isle of Avalon, for it is almost an island, being entirely surrounded

* MS. Arthurus.　　† MS. Wenneveria.　　‡ MS. Avallonia.

by marshes, whence it is named in British Inis* Avallon, that is the apple-bearing island, because apples (in British aval) used to abound in that place. Whence Morgan, a noblewoman who was ruler of that region and closely related to Arthur, after the Battle of Camlan† carried him away to the island now called Glastonbury to be healed of his wounds. It used also to be called in British Inis‡ Gutrin, that is, the isle of glass; hence the Saxons called it Glastingeburi. For in their tongue glas means glass,§ and a camp or town is called buri. We know that the bones of Arthur's body that were discovered were so large that in this we might see the fulfilment of the poet's words:

"Grandisque effossis mirabitur ossa sepulchris."‖

The thigh bone, when placed next to the tallest man present, as the abbot showed us, and fastened to the ground by his foot, reached three inches above his knee. And the skull was of a great, indeed prodigious, capacity, to the extent that the space between the brows and between the eyes was a palm's breadth. But in the skull there were ten or more wounds, which had all healed into scars with the exception of one, which made a great cleft, and seemed to have been the sole cause of death.'[7]

His account is confirmed in outline by Ralph of Coggeshall in his *Chronicon Anglicanum* some thirty years later:

'1191: This year were found at Glastonbury the bones of the most renowned Arthur, formerly King of Britain, buried in a very ancient coffin, over which two stone pyramids had been built: on the sides of these was an inscription, illegible on account of the rudeness of the script and its worn condition. The bones were discovered as follows:

* MS. enim.   † MS. Kemelen.   ‡ MS. eius.   § In Latin, vitrum.
‖ When the graves are opened, they shall marvel at the great size of the bones. (Virgil, *Georgics* I, 497.)

as they were digging up this ground to bury a monk who had urgently desired in his lifetime to be interred there, they discovered a certain coffin, on which a leaden cross had been placed, bearing the inscription "Here lies the famous king Arthur,* buried in the isle of Avalon.† For this place, which is surrounded by marshes, was formerly called the isle of Avalon, that is, the isle of apples.'[8]

But there is between the two versions an important discrepancy, which leads us to question the authenticity of the discovery. Giraldus Cambrensis quotes the words on the cross as 'Hic iacet sepultus inclytus rex Arthurus cum Wenneveria uxore sua secunda in insula Avallonia.' He repeats it in the *Speculum Ecclesiae*[9] twenty-five years later as: 'Hic iacet sepultus inclytus rex Arthurius in insula Avallonia cum uxore sua secunda Wenneveria.'‡ But Ralph of Coggeshall, although possibly relying on hearsay, while Giraldus had seen the cross himself, quotes words that agree more closely with later writers: 'Hic iacet inclitus rex Arturius, in insula Avallonis sepultus.' Bishop Ussher[10] in the seventeenth century quotes Leland as giving the inscription as: 'Hic iacet sepultus inclitus rex Arturius in insula Avalonia' from a copy of the original. He also gives from another source claiming to be an eyewitness description by one Simon of Abingdon the very different 'Hic iacet gloriosissimus rex Britonum Arturus.' Finally, Camden, from whose *Britannia* in the 1610 edition the illustration of the cross is taken, agrees with Leland and Ralph of Coggeshall: 'Hic iacet sepultus inclitus rex Arturius in insula Avalonia.'

What are we to make of this confusion? There is little doubt that Leland and Camden are quoting accurately what they saw on the copy of the cross which still existed in their day. Camden says of his illustration: '. . . which inscription or epitaph, as it

---

* MS. Arturius.   † MS. Avallonia.

‡ The description of Guinevere as his second wife may come from the legend of the true and false Guineveres, which is of Welsh origin, and was current at the time (cf. Vulgate Merlin, c. 1230).

was sometime exemplified and drawn out of the first copie in the Abbey of Glascon, I thought good for the antiquitie of the characters here to put downe. The letters being made after a barbarous maner, and resembling the Gothish Character, bewray plainly the barbarism of that age. . . .'

HIC IA
CET S
E PV
LTVS·IHCL
LTVS·S·REX
ARTV
RIV
S·IH
IHSV
LA·A
VALO
HI
A

It is clearly stated that the cross in Glastonbury Abbey is the 'first copie'. If he means by this the original cross, then our earliest witness is strangely inaccurate; it is far more probable that this is a second version, in which case deliberate alterations have been made. It is possible that awkward questions had been asked about the original, which exposed it as more recent than it claimed to be, and hence it was replaced by the one Camden and Leland saw shortly after the beginning of the thirteenth century. If this assumption be correct, the burial was staged by the Glastonbury monks.

When we turn to the other aspects of the question, this suspicion is confirmed. There is confusion over the dating: Giraldus Cambrensis in his first account gives no actual year; but in his second, he says that it was in the reign of Henry II which ended in July 1189, and in the abbacy of Henry of Sully, appointed in the following autumn! Ralph of Coggeshall puts it in 1191, two years later; although the news would scarcely have travelled so slowly as this, a year earlier might be possible without contradicting directly his evidence. Adam of Domerham gives it as 648 years after Arthur's death, which, if he followed Geoffrey of Monmouth's date for the battle of Camlan, would be 1190. This is a peculiar lack of consistency over a recent date, even though medieval chronicles are never exceptionally accurate.

A large number of forgeries of charters and other documents, as well as the interpolations in William of Malmesbury's *De Antiquitate Glastoniae*, which are now generally recognized as such, but which have long confused the issue, date from this decade onwards. The interpolations, which apparently make the claim that Arthur was buried at Glastonbury before the exhumation of 1190 confirmed it, are now dated at about 1250. As to the details of the actual digging, Adam of Domerham,[11] writing the Abbey history a century later, with access to Abbey records, may have unintentionally given us the final clue as to the true nature of the incident when he says that on the day the work began, the spot was surrounded by curtains on the abbot's orders.

Nor is a good motive for such a forgery lacking. Arthur's grave was an obvious attraction for pilgrims, and pilgrims were the abbey's chief source of income apart from its properties. They were the only way by which large additional sums could be made; and there was need of extra funds. In 1184, the buildings had been largely burnt down; but Henry II had provided the money for reconstruction. However, when he died in 1189 and Richard came to the throne, the Exchequer's resources were directed entirely to the fitting-out of the Crusade, and the supply of funds ceased. It is strange that within a few months of this, a new source of revenue should suddenly appear. Politically too, it would suit Richard; for the hope of Arthur's return could be used to foment rebellion in Wales, and this discovery seemed to dispose of it. Giraldus tells us that Henry told the monks something about Arthur being buried at Glastonbury; this may be an oblique reference to a hint from Henry that such a discovery would suit him for this reason.

Any discussion of the Glastonbury burial will, inevitably, like discussion of the historical Arthur, end without definite conclusion being reached. But the circumstantial evidence seems strong enough for us to say that there is not much doubt that the coffin and its contents, or at least its connection with Arthur, were produced by the monks in order to raise the money for the rebuilding of the Abbey, which, forgery or no forgery, it certainly did. Nor need all medieval monks be regarded as better in this respect than their secular contemporaries.

The last argument in favour of the interpretation set out above is the persistence of the Breton hope in its original form for another century or more, even after the influence of the Glastonbury story had led to alterations in the romances. William of Rennes, to whom a *Gesta Regum Britanniae* is attributed, of about 1250, mentions the tradition as though it were still current. Robert of Gloucester, in about 1290, prefers the Glastonbury story, but leaves little doubt that the other version still had its adherents. Some ten years later, Peter Langtoft takes a neutral view, saying he is not sure whether Arthur still lives or not. Robert Mannyng of Brunne calls it the 'Breton lye' writing in 1338. Our last trace of it is in Jehan de Wavrin's chronicle of about 1400, where it seems to be a dead tradition. Surely, if Glastonbury's Arthur were genuine, the old stories which gave quite different accounts of his end would not have taken two hundred years to die.

It is possible that another reason for choosing to 'discover' Arthur was that Glastonbury had already been equated with Avalon. In 1136, it was known to the Welsh as Inis Gutrin (Isle of Glass).[12] And among the Welsh other-worlds was an Isle of Glass, which appears in the poem *The Spoils of Annwfn* already mentioned. Its climate, like that of Avalon in the *Vita Merlini*, was remarkably mild. Both Glastonbury and this Isle of Glass were associated with Melwas. There were connections enough to enable Glastonbury to be identified as Avalon.[13]

Even after 1400 belief in Arthur's return still recurs. But it has passed into the realms of folklore; some stories describe him as wandering in the form of a bird, usually a Cornish chough, or a raven. Most of these tales conform to a definite type, that of the sleeping warrior who will one day reappear as leader when called by the breaking of a spell.[14] Such stories have been told of every great national hero, and are readily adaptable to new names and characters as events provide them. The earliest appearance of Arthur in this role is recorded in Gervase of Tilbury's *Otia Imperialia*, about 1210. The writer knows the current Avalon version, but also describes the recent adventure of the groom of an Italian bishop, who, while following a stray horse on Mount Etna, came across Arthur in a sort of Earthly Paradise, entered by a cleft in the rock. There are other, similar stories of Arthur and Etna of this period, probably due to Norman influence in Sicily.

In Britain, there are two important versions of the story, the best known being attached to Craig-y-Dinas near Snowdon and some other Welsh caves. There is also a non-Arthurian version from Swaffham in Norfolk. On London Bridge, a Welshman with a hazel staff meets a stranger who tells him that a treasure lies hidden under the tree from which the staff was cut. They return together to Wales, and find the tree, and a cave beneath it. In the passage leading to the cave hangs a bell which must on no account be touched. If it rings, the warriors in the cave, among whom is Arthur, waiting to lead the Welsh to their former glory, will awake and ask: 'Is it day?' The answer must be: 'No, sleep thou on.' This happens: but the correct answer is given, and the Welshman is able to take some of the treasure. On his next visit, he forgets the formula, and is beaten until he is crippled by the warriors. He is never able to find the cave again.

The other version is found at Sewingshields on the Roman

wall, and at Richmond. The visitor finds Arthur and Guinevere and his court sleeping by a table on which lie a garter, a sword and a bugle. The garter must be cut and the horn blown, at which Arthur will arise and lead the Britons to victory. But the visitor only does the first and Arthur awakes only to fall asleep again. The Richmond version concerns one Potter Thompson, who is dismissed with these words by Arthur:

> 'Potter Thompson, Potter Thompson, hadst thou blown
> the horn,
> Thou hadst been the greatest man that ever was born.'

A similar rhyme is used at Sewingshields. Other northern localities have similar stories; as with the Welsh legend the place-name was changed by each story-teller. Cadbury in Somerset also claims to be Arthur's sleeping-place, although he has never been seen there. It was here in about 1880 that the incident told by Dean Robinson[15] took place. A visiting party of antiquaries were asked by an old man living near by whether they had 'come to take away the king'. So within the last century memories of Arthur's expected and eagerly awaited return were still alive, fifteen hundred years after his death. It is only in this latest and most sceptical age that Arthur has really died.

A genealogical chart of the sources of Malory's Arthurian romances.

- Geoffrey of Monmouth
  - Gaimar (1)
  - Wace
    - Layamon
      - Verse *Morte Arthure*
      - Verse Chronicles *Arthur*
    - Chrétien de Troyes
      - Continuators
        - Percyvelle of Galles
        - Ywain and Gawain
        - Ieaste of Sir Gawayne

- Breton and Celtic sources
  - Marie de France
    - *Sir Launfal*
  - Thomas of Britain
    - *Sir Tristrem*
  - Other French Writers
    - *Sir Gawain and the Carl of Carlisle*
    - Wedding of Sir Gawain
    - *Sir Libeaus Desconus*
    - *Sir Gawain and the Green Knight*
    - *Turk and Gawain*
    - *Prose Tristan*

- Robert de Boron
  - The Vulgate Cycle
    - Estoire del St. Graal
    - E. de Merlin
      - *Arthour and Merlin*
    - *Livres de Lancelot*
      - Lancelot du Lak
    - *Queste del St. Graal*
      - *La Mort Artu*
        - *Le Morte Arthur*
  - Pseudo-Robert-de-Boron Cycle
    - E. del St. Graal
    - *Merlin* Huth MS
    - Queste
    - Mort Arthur

LEGEND

—— English Romances
italic Malory's Sources
(1) Original lost

FIVE

THE EARLIEST ENGLISH POEMS

WE have seen Arthur in many guises so far: as military commander, petty tyrant, and as emperor. But none of these is his familiar role; nor have we met more than a handful of the figures we usually associate with him and his court; Gawain, Lancelot, Perceval, Galahad and Tristram have only appeared briefly, if at all. On the other hand, we have not yet studied any complete literary work with Arthur or his court as its central connecting thread. The first such work that has come down to us dates from 750 years after the death of the historical Arthur; but once this dormant period was over, and Arthur had aroused the interest of poets as a possible literary hero, his establishment in this new part took hardly fifty years.

These two contrasting periods, the one of protracted inactivity, the other of intense creativity, make the progress of Arthur from history to literature complicated and obscure. Let us retrace our steps before we study his adventures in this new realm. Arthur the warrior was a hero shared by three branches of the Celtic race, all descendants of the Britons whom he led into battle: the Bretons, the Welsh, and the Cornish. The Welsh developed his story to the greatest extent, and preserved the spark of memory. At some time early in the twelfth century the imagination of the Bretons was fired by it, and they embroidered Arthur's exploits after their own fashion, spreading their recited tales into France.

F   65

Here the poets received them attentively, and fanned the flame into a blaze that swept Europe from Iceland to Greece.

The Bretons who brought the stories into France were probably minstrels, and their versions would have been in prose. Their plots were simple in outline, filled out by incidents which were only distantly connected with the main story. Such incidents supplanted to a large extent the long lists of heroes which recur so often in the Welsh by marvellous adventures in which knights took part, and made the material more attractive to the French. It is not unreasonable to suppose that it was the French who introduced some of the more subtle traits of the romances. The content of the Breton prose was put into the more expressive medium of verse: the incidents were woven more closely into the plot; and the centre of interest moved from the events of the tale to its characters.

Chrétien de Troyes is the first writer definitely known to have carried out this process of refinement. He was born at Troyes, and was well educated, for he shows an extensive knowledge of classical literature. He moved in aristocratic circles, and it was at the court of Comtesse Marie de Champagne that most of his work was produced. The exact dates of his period of activity are hard to fix, but seem to have been between 1170, ten years after Marie became countess, and about 1185.

His first Arthurian work, *Erec*, was probably based on one of the Breton stories, which he improved in the fashion outlined above. This was followed by *Cligès*, an entirely original work composed of various conventional situations. He returned to Celtic tradition with the *Chevalier de la Charrette*, in which Lancelot makes his first appearance in literature; this was commissioned by Comtesse Marie. *Yvain, ou le Chevalier au Lion*, part tradition, part invention, followed; of this we shall have more to say later. Chrétien then turned away from Arthurian stories to write a pious narrative about William the Conqueror, *Guillaume d'Angleterre*. Finally, at the request of Count Philippe of Alsace, the 'Perceval' or *Conte del Graal* was begun. But

Chrétien died before completing it, and as a result the Grail's origin is much less clear than it might have been, for the two writers who tried in succession to complete the *Conte del Graal* never knew Chrétien's intentions, and were forced to invent their own idea of the Grail.[1] The *Conte del Graal* was begun after 1181 and not later than 1190, for in that year Count Philippe departed for the Holy Land, and never returned.[2] So Chrétien probably died in the last decade of the twelfth century.

Chrétien's once enormous appeal is not readily seen by the reader of today: the stories, stripped of the aura of mystery given to them by the Celts, tend to become pure extravaganzas, in which adventure follows adventure without any logical sequence or apparent meaning, even though connected by the figure of the hero. But this is his inheritance from the Bretons: his own work, in which the finest part of these romances lies, is the introspective psychology of his characters. The narrative is only the pretext for the heart-searchings, anguished and joyful, of his heroes and heroines. This loose connection of his plot with his real theme is emphasized by his introduction of many small but realistic details that interest him; the rituals of medieval everyday life and the ways of love fall equally under his penetrating gaze. But even if the adventures are never the most important part of his works, as they became in later writers, it does not mean that he despised them or never realized their possibilities. As one would expect, it is merely that he preferred courtly love to knightly adventures; in his hands, this idea becomes more than an abstraction, and appears as a natural and practical part of life. Although the first writer in this new genre, he is also in many ways its greatest exponent.

In his five romances, Chrétien covers most of the story of Arthur, apart from the parts based on the *Historia Regum Britanniae*. Here are Lancelot and Perceval, Gawain and Kay, in much the same roles as in Malory. But one major branch of the Arthurian legend is not his: the tragedy of Tristan and Iseult. Although in *Cligès* he claims to have written of Mark and Iseult and many other noble tales,[3] it is believed that the original of the finest of many Arthurian love-stories was written a decade before *Erec*.[4] Arthur and his court only appear incidentally in the earlier versions, and it might well be thought that it was only later added to the cycle. Yet such evidence as we have, including a curious Welsh triad that mentions Arthur, Kay, Bedivere, Tristram and Iseult, in a raid on Mark's piggeries,* suggests that the association goes back to the Celtic legends. Two versions of the story that are roughly contemporary with Chrétien have survived, one by Béroul, the other by Thomas of Britain; they have many features in common and evidently derive from a common lost original. The 'lais', short poems relating only a single incident, refer to the story in terms which bear witness to its wide popularity. In general, the same is true of the early versions of the Tristram legend as of Chrétien's works. Their simplicity and unity makes them less confusing and hence more attractive to us today than the vastly more diffuse later romances.

The French writers after 1190† did not follow Chrétien's lead entirely; they preferred to omit his reflection of contemporary life and analysis of love, in order to concentrate on the adventures and marvels. The first works after Chrétien were the two continuations of his *Conte del Graal* already mentioned. The writers who were active shortly after his death considerably enlarged the material of the Arthurian legend, drawing on their own imagination and on Celtic sources, until it evolved into a cyclical form, the framework of which was formed by the histories of the Grail and of Arthur himself. The first of these cycles is in verse, and is ascribed in the manuscripts to Robert de Boron. From this developed the fullest connected, though hardly unified, version of the Arthurian romances in any language, that contained in the Vulgate Cycle. Its final form was established between 1220 and 1230, and was divided into five branches, in prose. It opens with the *Estoire del Graal* (*Story of the Grail*),

* This episode recurs in John Masefield's play *Tristan and Isolt*.
† See Appendix.

which describes the adventures of the Grail up to its arrival in Britain, and which forms a prelude to the fourth branch. The second branch, the *Estoire de Merlin* (*Story of Merlin*) relates Merlin's and Arthur's births, and Arthur's military career. This is an elaborate revision of the original history in Geoffrey of Monmouth's *Historia Regum Britanniae*. Next comes the *Livres de Lancelot* (*Book of Lancelot*), containing the main body of knightly adventures. The *Queste del Saint Graal* (*Quest of the Holy Grail*) deals with the search for the Grail and its achievement; it is evolved from the *Conte del Graal* of Chrétien already mentioned. The fifth and last branch *La Mort Artu* (*The Death of Arthur*) relates the final disintegration of the Round Table and the civil wars against Lancelot and Mordred.

There are, however, some variations. One of these omits the *Livres de Lancelot*, but includes an extension of the second branch called the *Suite de Merlin* (*Sequel of Merlin*) which is designed as a prelude to the last two branches. Another variant was never actually included in the Vulgate Cycle, but might well have been; this is the *Prose Tristan*, longer than any of the five branches, whose nucleus was the Tristram and Iseult story. On to this were grafted large sections of the *Livres de Lancelot*, with the result that the interludes make the framework fall apart, and this becomes the most unwieldy of the prose romances.

Yet these vast compilations are not, as has sometimes been assumed, even by competent critics, mere amassments of incident, which fall into easily distinguished sections, even though their length makes any unity obscure. A recent writer[5] has emphasized their tapestry-like quality; the themes are interwoven in such a way that, while they do not form a definitely ordered and logically unified whole, they have a subtle conjunction of recurrent characters or stories, and the skill with which this is sometimes done is the great quality of their composers' art. Virtually every incident has a precedent and a consequence; even the frame of the Cycle conforms to this rule, since the opening branch is the precedent for the *Queste del Saint Graal*, and in the variant form, the *Suite de Merlin* foreshadows both the *Queste* and *La Mort Artu*.

Even so, the final versions of these cycles was so enlarged by multiplication of themes that it was almost impossible to read them as a whole. When Sir Thomas Malory began his tales ' drawn from the French ', he rapidly realized the need for drastic abridgement and omission, and his work is adaptation rather than translation. The main period of innovation ended in France by 1250, and although the works remained popular well into the fifteenth century, there were no important new productions after this date.

England owes most of its romances to France, and the remainder are native inventions. Hence the great Arthurian writers of Germany had no influence on English literature until the nineteenth century, and even then they contributed no more than details. But their work is in many ways superior to the bulk of the French, for the single romance was favoured, with a more integral plot, and none of the excesses of the cycles appear. The Grail and the story of Tristram and Iseult were the basis of the two masterpieces produced in Germany, Wolfram von Eschenbach's *Parzival* and Gottfried von Strassburg's *Tristan*. Both turn away from the physical and sensual aspect of courtly love which dominates the French concept of it, and replace it with a mystical ideal, such as it had originally been. In *Parzival*, the hero's fidelity to his lady, Kondwiramurs, is contrasted with Gawain's easier morals; and Tristan and Isolde rise above the sensual to find greater joys in a spiritual love. This reconciliation of the Christian ideal in Arthurian legend typified by the Grail, and of *amour courtois*, typified by Lancelot and Guinevere, was never achieved in the French cycles, and was to lead Malory into difficult contradiction and confusion when he tried to present a consistent version of the latter.

Direct translations from the French, numerous enough already, continued to flourish for another two centuries after 1250, and almost every European language acquired a story or two about

Arthur in this way. In some instances, this has preserved for us works now lost in the original, notably Thomas of Britain's version of the Tristram legend, of which there has survived an almost complete Scandinavian version. A Dutch romance preserves an otherwise completely unknown story about a son of Gawain; but, considering the number of romances that are sometimes supposed to have been lost, there is remarkably little that is entirely new in these translations, compared with the numerous versions of works whose original has come down to us.

Having thus outlined the Continental developments, we may return to England. The earliest of the English romances was composed at about the time when the French activity ceased, half-way through the thirteenth century, and the last is twenty years later than Malory's 'noble tales'; thus they cover a span of 250 years, from 1250 to 1500. None of them is on the same scale of size as their French counterparts, and of the twenty-three known to us, there are only five original works. Four derive from lost French sources, and the remaining eighteen have known originals; of the latter, five are direct English renderings of complete French works.

The products of the English writers are usually inferior to their French parallels, whose courtly and polished style, with its leisurely rate of progress, is invariably shortened and simplified. They are chiefly the work of humbler writers or of amateurs, who only rarely managed to realize the innate dramatic or psychological potential of the stories they were telling. This lack of great English masterpieces is, in the main, due to a lack of demand for poems on a high literary level; for the upper classes could read the French in the original, and only when the romances were waning in popularity was there any demand from such quarters for translations. So when we do come to the one masterpiece of our native medieval Arthurian literature, *Sir Gawain and the Green Knight*, its splendours impress us all the more deeply.

Only the dramatic simplicity of the English romances saves them from total oblivion, and this all too often becomes banality. There is a complete contrast with the psychological refinement and leisurely pace of the French, usually because they were intended for recital rather than reading, and the introspective soliloquies of Chrétien's heroes and heroines were scarcely adapted to the minstrel's art. In any case, they were composed in response to the audience's demand for adventures and marvels, and had to be direct. The sort of verse that this produced was at best the battle scenes of the *Morte Arthure,** and at worst the doggerel lines of *The Green Knight*. Most of the abridgement of the stories is also due to the influence of the minstrels, for none of the original or largely original poems is more than 1,000 lines in length, and they usually deal with isolated incidents.

With this simplification goes a marked lack of taste and sophistication. Love is little discussed, and the physical side of it is more in evidence than the psychological. The wealth of kings and princes, on the other hand, is not tacitly assumed or indicated in a discreet phrase, but is described with obvious amazement and wonder. The exaggerated and grotesque is greatly-favoured; giants and monsters are preferred to ordinary human beings as the target of adventures.[6]

In order to simplify the study of the romances, it is usual to divide them into seven groups. Of these, one—romances with Gawain as hero—will be discussed in the next chapter, as they are so numerous in proportion to the others as to warrant a separate survey. The first group must obviously be that of which Arthur is the central figure. His birth and early career are the subject of three romances, and a further poem relates personal exploits of his. Here we are not so far from the original chronicler's story, and we shall return to it in the group of poems dealing with the close of his life.

---

* *Sir Gawain and the Green Knight* was written for a more literate audience. See next chapter.

Arthour and Merlin[7] is one of the earliest English composi-
tions, dating from the second half of the thirteenth century. It is
one of a group of three romances written in Kent at about this
time, and is one of the longest poems we have; even though
incomplete, it is just under 10,000 lines in all. As its title implies, it has much to say about Merlin as well, and the first part
deals with his career up to Uther's succession to the throne in
considerable detail. We need only note that this account comes
almost directly from the French Vulgate Cycle.

The first 'fytte' of the second part opens with a description of
Uther's exploits under Merlin's guidance, which include the
overthrow of Hengist and the defeat of the Saxons. The begetting
of Arthur is told in similar fashion to the story in the *Historia
Regum Britanniae*, except that the child is put in the care of Sir
Antour, on Merlin's advice. Uther dies, without revealing the
existence of his son, and an assembly is summoned to choose a
successor. However, before a decision is reached, a sword fixed
in a stone appears mysteriously in a churchyard. The inscription
on it says that whoever draws it out is the rightful overlord of
Britain. Uther's allies attempt to do so, but it is not until
Arthur lays his hand to its hilt that the sword yields. Merlin
then arrives and explains the mysterious events.

Arthur naturally arouses some enmity between himself and
the rival claimants, and his coronation is followed by a battle
between him and the kings who have rebelled against him. The
latter are driven out of Carlisle, but immediately lay siege to it.
Merlin puts them to flight, and advises Arthur to seek King Ban
and King Bors of France as allies. With these additional forces,
and Merlin's ever-helpful magic, he succeeds in defeating the
rebels, who submit, unwillingly, to his suzerainty.

However, the Saxons have taken advantage of these internal
discords to renew their attacks, and Arthur now has to defeat
them as well. With assistance from various other quarters, he
drives them out of his own kingdom, although even then they by
no means leave Britain, but merely harass the kings who are his

vassals. Gawain and Galachin, sons of two of the formerly rebellious kings, are foremost among his helpers. Gawain has the peculiar property that his strength is doubled until noon: normal between then and three o'clock: and again doubled until dusk. These two encounter and defeat various units of the enemy on their way to London, and arrive safely to relieve their father.

Meanwhile, Arthur is at Carohais, with Merlin and a bodyguard of thirty-nine knights. Here he offers his services to King Leodegrance, who is being besieged by King Ryence of North Wales. The following day, the latter attacks with 60,000 men. After an initial success gained by Arthur, Leodegrance is captured. Merlin effects his rescue, but, although Arthur's own contingent is victorious, the main body of the army is driven back against the city wall. The tide is only turned when Arthur kills the leader of the enemy, one Saphiran, whereupon the remainder make a final effort, and only 500 Saxons return to King Ryence. Arthur now meets Guinevere, Leodegrance's daughter, for the first time. She has an illegitimate half-sister of the same name, who resembles her closely, but Arthur is able to distinguish between the true and false Guineveres and falls in love with the true one.

The misfortunes of the rebellious kings are now dealt with in detail. Most of them have suffered severely at the hands of the Saxons, but Gawain, who has remained in London, defeats some of the latter, with the aid of a certain Sir Sagremore of Hungary. Others are discomfited by Ywain and his half-brother of the same name, sons of another of the rebellious kings. The Saxons, however, turn northward, and overthrow Lot, Gawain's father, but a swift revenge is taken by Gawain, and the Saxons are virtually expelled from Britain. There is a momentary lull in the campaigns, and Merlin rejoins Arthur, having directed the foregoing operations under various disguises. Arthur is now betrothed to Guinevere.

However, further campaigning is necessary, and the last canto describes the battle in which Ryence is finally discomfited. After

some spell-casting from Merlin, the two armies clash; the outcome is for a long time doubtful, but Arthur eventually succeeds
in severely wounding Ryence. The latter flees: but Merlin has to
extract Leodegrance from the difficulties he has got into before
the remainder of Ryence's army is slaughtered, and Arthur can
return with Leodegrance to Carohais. At this point the manuscript break off.

The sources for this work seem to have been a combination of
the French *Suite de Merlin* of the variant version of the Vulgate
Cycle mentioned earlier, with some sort of romantic chronicle of
Arthur's career. It contains a seemingly endless succession of
wars and battles, introducing many of the familiar heroes.
Gawain is especially prominent, and Mordred appears as
Arthur's nephew. As a whole, the plot suffers from excessive re-
petition, since some half-dozen campaigns are described in detail.

Its merit lies in some of the battle scenes, which are occasionally vigorous, although without the strength of the alliterative
poems. The lyrical passages, directly drawn from the French
original, are attractive: one of the finest is the description of
Guinevere arming Arthur before the final battle, which retains
something of the courtly atmosphere.

We have already spoken of Merlin's origins and Geoffrey of
Monmouth's contributions. From his magical powers, he became associated in later medieval legend outside the Arthurian
stories with the Antichrist, and this story appears in *Arthour and
Merlin*. However, the more common portrait is that of a 'white'
magician of benevolent designs. His association with Nimue and
eventual downfall are found in essence in the *Vita Merlini*, and
were used to emphasize his human qualities.

Another English writer—again, like the majority of the authors
we are concerned with, anonymous—has given us a close translation of the now lost source of *Arthour and Merlin*. The English
Prose Merlin continues the story up to the birth of Lancelot.
Slightly earlier in date than Malory's works, it has none of their
qualities.[8] Equally uninspired is the amateur verse translation of

the *Estoire de Merlin* branch of the French Vulgate Cycle by Henry Lovelich the skinner.[9] It was made *c.* 1450–60 for another member of the Skinner's Company, and the translator seems to have lost interest half-way through the work, for there is a decline in its already mediocre standard towards the end. He made no abridgements, and the total length is 28,000 lines. His version of the Grail story is equally tedious, and only covers the early part of the story, which is a piece of apocryphal religious history that has little to do with Arthur. One only wishes that one of the lost masterpieces of medieval literature had come down to us instead of these unreadable works.

The last poem in this group contains four adventures found nowhere else in Arthurian literature. Arthur himself is hero of one of them, as we learn from the title, *The Avowing of King Arthur, Sir Gawain, Sir Kay, and Sir Bawdewin of Britain.*[10] It is in northern dialect, of the middle of the fourteenth century, and is relatively short, being a little over 1,000 lines. The poem opens at Carlisle, where Arthur hears of a great boar near by, which with the help of the three knights of the title, he hunts to a lair in Inglewood forest. There they all make vows. Arthur is to kill the boar single-handed before dawn: Gawain is to watch all night at the haunted Tarn Wadeling: Kay is to ride through the forest until daybreak, and to slay anyone who tries to restrain him: Bawdewin swears never to be jealous of his wife or any other lady, never to refuse food to any man, and not to fear the threat of death.

Arthur kills the boar with much difficulty, cuts it up, and devoutly gives thanks to the Virgin. Kay is captured in an attempt to rescue a maiden, and is only to be released if Gawain will joust with his captor. Gawain does so at the Tarn Wadeling, and Kay's vanquisher, Sir Menealfe, is overthrown and sent to the Queen, who gives him to Arthur. He is made a knight of the Round Table. Bawdewin's valour is tested by five knights sent by the King; he successfully overthrows them. Similar tests are applied to his hospitality and to his faith in his wife, all of which prove his worth, and the poem ends with Bawdewin's explanation of the events in his life which led him to make the triple vow.

This story has no immediate known sources, but the vows made by the four knights are paralleled in what may be termed the 'literature of boasting'; another (fragmentary) Arthurian example is *King Arthur and King Cornwall*. Those vows are used to good effect by the English writer to give a series of knightly adventures a real unity rarely achieved in the romances. The style is unrefined but otherwise good.

The characters and places in it are common to two other stories of similar origin, the *Awntyrrs of Arthur* and *The Wedding of Sir Gawain*. In all three, Tarn Wadeling (or Wathelin), Carlisle, and Inglewood Forest occur. It is conceivable that in their original form all three were by the same hand, although the extant versions are widely divergent in construction and style. It is equally possible that these place-names were borrowed by the later of the three writers.

The first two knights of the title, Gawain and Kay, are familiar enough, but the fourth, Sir Bawdewin or Baldwin, is not mentioned in any French work, and Malory introduces him from some other source. We find him, however, in two other English poems whose tone is not very different from the present one, *The Turk and Gawain*, and *Sir Gawain and the Carl of Carlisle*, where he is a bishop, and not a very Christian one at that. But the bishop seems to have preceded the knight, and his secularization was probably accidental, for in the *Mabinogi* we find a bishop by the name of Bedwini.

Romances with a single hero form the bulk of the Middle English works. We have already said that Gawain has so many attached to his name that we must devote a whole chapter to them. The next figure we come to is that of Perceval, whom only one poem commemorates, and that not of great merit. Yet *Sir Perceval of Galles* *[11] presents some interesting features. Con-

* 'of Wales'.

temporary with *The Avowing of King Arthur*, it is also from the North, but is about twice as long.

Perceval, father of the hero, a famous knight of Arthur's court, weds Arthur's sister Acheflour. During the jousts in the wedding celebrations, he severely wounds the Red Knight, who swears to avenge himself. Perceval and Acheflour have a son, in whose honour a tournament is held. Here the Red Knight gains his revenge by killing Perceval. Acheflour swears that she will never let her son be trained in knightly skills lest he meet a similar fate. She retires to a forest retreat with him, where she brings him up and calls him after his father. One day, however, as he is hunting deer, he meets three knights from Arthur's court, Ywain, Gawain and Kay. He asks which of them is God, about whom his mother has recently told him, and threatens to kill them if they do not answer. Kay laughs at him, but Gawain rebukes him, and explains. He immediately wants Arthur to make him a knight, but Gawain has doubts as to this. He returns to his mother, finding a horse on the way, which he rides bareback. She is much dismayed by his story when he arrives, and realizes that she cannot restrain him. She gives him a ring by which she will be able to recognize him, and he departs.

He comes to a hall on his way to the court, where in accordance with his mother's counsel of moderation, he decides to take only half of all that he sees. He finds a lady sleeping there and exchanges his ring for hers. On arrival at Arthur's palace, he rides straight into the banqueting hall where the king is at meat. Arthur recognizes him as his nephew, and bids him sit down in response to his request for knighthood. The meal is suddenly interrupted by the entry of the Red Knight, who seizes the King's cup, drains it, and carries it off. Perceval sets out, in pursuit, kills the Red Knight, and is about to burn the body in order to get the armour, when Gawain comes up and shows him how to undo it. He gives Gawain the cup but refuses to return himself. Instead he continues on his way, in the Red Knight's armour, and mounted on his horse. After various adventures he meets a messenger from a lady in distress, who has been sent to seek help from Arthur against a certain Soudan who is besieging her. Perceval offers his services, but the messenger insists on going to Arthur. Undaunted, Perceval sets out in quest of the Soudan. The messenger arrives at court, and Arthur, Ywain, Gawain and Kay depart in search of Perceval, who has already disposed of many of the Soudan's men. When Arthur and his companions arrive at the siege, Perceval, thinking that the Soudan is among them, attacks them, but Gawain recognizes him, and all is well. He then kills the Soudan, and weds the lady of the castle, Lufamour. But he remembers his mother, and in spite of Lufamour's entreaties, goes in search of her. He comes across a lady bound to a tree, and after releasing her, asks why she had been thus punished. She tells him that her husband, the Black Knight, had done it, because someone had exchanged rings with her without her knowledge, and he suspects her of infidelity. Perceval realizes that she is the sleeping lady he had visited earlier, and defeats the Black Knight. He explains to the latter, whereupon the pair are reconciled. Unfortunately the ring given to Perceval by his mother has come into the possession of a neighbouring giant, whom Perceval has to find and kill. He obtains the ring from the giant's porter, but is told that on account of it, the lady the giant loved had accused her suitor of killing her son, and had gone mad. She was living in the woods near by. Perceval realizes that this must be Acheflour his mother, and at last finds her. She recovers from her madness and goes to live with him and his bride. Later in life, Perceval goes on a Crusade to the Holy Land, where he is killed.

The most arresting point of this otherwise not very unusual story is that it is the only known poem in which Perceval is in no way connected with the Grail. The earliest romance of which he is hero is Chrétien de Troyes's unfinished *Conte del Graal*, which tells a story of Perceval's boyhood in very similar terms, but introduces the Grail at the end of it. Thus from the very beginning this connection has existed; but the great question is whether the

English romance in fact represents the original form of the story, to which the Grail was later attached, or whether it is a later adaptation of Chrétien's work.

Once again, there are two opposing schools of thought on the problem. The first, headed by Miss J. L. Weston[12] and A. C. L. Brown[13] sees in the English romance a late form of the original of Chrétien's poem, which the latter believes to have been an Anglo-Norman version of the Irish *Boyish Exploits of Finn*, without any mention of the Grail story, although features in the Irish tale could have encouraged such an association. The opposing view was taken by Professor J. D. Bruce,[14] namely, that the English writer, finding a copy of Chrétien's work without the continuations, proceeded to adapt it, leaving out the Grail, since, in the unfinished form it is not clear what is intended by the Grail itself, and he may have been at a loss to conclude the story logically.

To discuss the pros and cons of this argument is outside the scope of the present work, since it would involve a further long excursion into continental romance. The curious reader may follow up the subject for himself from the references given, but it will suffice for the moment to say that the previous view is now generally accepted. An Italian poem, *Carduino*, preserves a similar story, without the Grail, and seems to have been derived from a French source similar to the English poem. The style of the latter is so far removed from that of Chrétien that it must be argued that a romance was in circulation which told the story of Perceval's youthful deeds only, and was earlier than the *Conte del Graal*.

The poem as it stands is a straightforward example of a theme which recurs several times in Arthurian literature: a simpleton arrives at court with some outrageous request, is laughed at by some of the knights, but much to their surprise, performs great feats, and sometimes defeats those who mocked him. Another romance, *Sir Libeaus Desconus*, and Malory's *Tale of Gareth*, tell a similar story, in which a newly-made knight is sent, at his own request, on an adventure with a maiden who scorns him; he performs many feats of arms for her, but only gets rebukes, until the maiden herself is in turn rebuked for her harshness by a knight he has overthrown. Parallels to it may be found in folklore of all the Celtic races. The Irish example quoted is the closest known.

The poem itself has no merits. Its minstrel tone is ill-suited to a work of such length, and it has none of the smoothness of *Ywain and Gawain*. Even though the object of the translator is little more than to tell a succession of marvels such as appealed to popular taste, he does not really carry it out effectively. The homely tone is probably accidental, but it is the only point of the style which is appropriate. Were it not for the unusual form of the Perceval story which it contains, the romance would deserve no more than a passing reference.

There are only two Middle English versions of the Grail legend other than Malory's and neither is of great interest. *Joseph of Arimathie*,[15] a Midland romance of *c.* 1350, is really outside the Arthurian legend, since it comes from the early part of the first branch of the Vulgate Cycle, and has no connections with later events, as it is a brief excerpt of only 709 verses. It has considerable dignity and simplicity and is one of the earlier Middle English alliterative poems.

Of all the Arthurian stories, that of Tristram and Iseult is the most moving and dramatic. It was thought for some considerable time that an Anglo-Norman poet, Thomas of Britain, was responsible for the original, thus accrediting to an English poet a romance of really major importance even though he wrote in French. However, as we have seen, it is now believed that he shared a common lost source with Béroul, a contemporary French writer.

The sources of this lost romance have been exhaustively investigated.[16] The historical Drust, a Pictish chieftain of the eighth century, had several adventures attached to his name in Welsh legend. Using him as hero, the main body of the romance

G

is paralleled in the Irish stories of Diarmuid and Grainne, of Nasi and Deirdre, and of Arthed. The *Wooing of Emer* presents further similarities. In the Breton lai of *Eliduc* we find the story of the man loved by two women of the same name, probably of oriental origin. The love potion is found in classical literature, as is the final incident of the black and white sails, taken from the Theseus legend. This would imply a writer with a very wide knowledge of such stories, but it is conceivable that the Irish and Breton tales were gathered in a Cornish form, which would explain the place-names, and the romancer then further embellished this version, chiefly from classical and continental sources.

Thomas of Britain's poem[17] so far as we can judge, differs little from the original. We possess it only in a reconstructed form, which is none the less close enough to give us an idea of his style and imagery, as it is based on a direct translation into Norse of some four or five decades later. It has the usual traits of the early French romances: interest in psychology and character and a leisurely pace.

The only Middle English version, *Sir Tristrem*,[18] has fallen greatly in esteem since Sir Walter Scott edited it and wrote a completion in 1804. It was held by him to be the original of the story, Thomas of Ercildoune being identical with Thomas of Britain. It is 3,344 verses in length, in a curious jingling metre of which the writer was evidently very proud. The dialect is northern, and it was composed about 1290.

Tristram's father, Roland Riis, is engaged in mortal strife with Morgan. He comes to King Mark's court to take part in a tournament, and falls in love with Blancheflour, the king's sister. He is victorious in the lists, although wounded. But Morgan breaks the truce that had been declared for the duration of his absence, and Roland has to return in haste. However, Blancheflour accompanies him, and they are married on arrival at Roland's lands. In the ensuing war, Roland is killed; Blancheflour dies in giving birth to Tristram, who is brought up by Sir Rohant as his own son.

He is taught the usual knightly arts, and becomes especially skilled in hunting. One day a Norwegian ship comes to Rohant's shore, and Tristram gets involved in a game of chess with the captain for a wager. He wins; but the captain, instead of paying him, sets sail with him still on board. After nine weeks, they run into a storm, and the sailors, being superstitious, give him his winnings, and head for the land to put him ashore. The weather clears and he lands safely.

The first people he meets are a group of huntsmen, cutting up their quarry in what seems to him a very crude fashion. He shows them how it should be done according to the laws of venery, and goes with them to King Mark's court, for he is now in Cornwall. Mark has heard nothing from his sister and brother-in-law, and hence, when the stranger tells him he is Sir Rohant's son, he sees no connection between Tristram and himself. However Rohant arrives at Mark's court in search of Tristram, and, by means of a ring given to him by Blancheflour, identifies him as Mark's nephew. Tristram learns of his father's fate, and kills Morgan, giving his lands to Rohant before settling at Tintagel. On his return he finds Mark in downcast mood for the annual tribute to Anguish of Ireland is due, unless a challenger can be found to meet the Irish champion Moraunt. Tristram offers to do this, and kills Moraunt, but is himself severely wounded. His pain is such that he cannot bear company, and he sets sail alone, intending to drift about until he dies. The ship is driven on to the Irish coast. Here he lands, and realizing he is liable to be killed by Moraunt's kin, adopts the name Tramtrist, saying that he is a merchant who has been attacked by pirates. The Queen, Moraunt's sister, heals his wounds, and he sees Iseult for the first time.

He stays in Ireland for a year, and then returns to King Mark, who is now seeking a wife. Tristram describes Iseult's beauty, and offers to fetch her for him. He finds Dublin terrified by a dragon, which he proceeds to slay, although he is again wounded. The Queen once more heals him, but Iseult discovers his true identity, and but for the Queen's intervention, would have killed him. He then reveals his mission and persuades her to return with him to Cornwall, accompanied by her lady, Brangwain. On the voyage, Brangwain accidentally gives them the love-potion intended for Mark's wedding night, and henceforth they are eternally inseparable.

Iseult duly marries Mark, but Tristram remains her lover. Soon afterwards, an Irish harper comes to the court, and so delights Mark with his playing, that the King grants him whatever he desires. He chooses the queen; but Tristram rescues her and restores her to Mark. In spite of suspicion cast on them by other members of the court, Tristram remains in Mark's favour for three years, but at the end of this time his guilt is proved, and he has to flee. He returns to Iseult disguised as a beggar, just before she is to be tried for infidelity, and carries her down to the ship in full view of the court. Iseult is able to swear that none save the king has been closer to her than this beggar.

Tristram, after killing Morgan's brother, succeeds in regaining Mark's favour for a time, only to be driven away again, this time with the Queen. Neither finds this a great hardship. Mark discovers them asleep one day while he is out hunting, with a naked sword lying between them. He takes this as final proof of their innocence, and they return; yet once more their enemies find evidence against them, and Tristram leaves for Spain. After various adventures there, he comes to Brittany, where he weds Iseult of the White Hands. A glimpse of the other Iseult's ring on his wedding night reminds him of her faithfulness, and Iseult of Brittany, although his wife, remains a virgin.

Tristram then defeats the giant Beliagog, who has been disturbing the King of Brittany, and makes him build a hall in honour of Iseult of Ireland and Brangwain. Tristram's extraordinary conduct towards Iseult of the White Hands is discovered by her brother Ganhardin, who is then let into the secret. On seeing a portrait of Brangwain he declares that he must see her in the flesh or die, and he and Tristram set out for

Cornwall, where Iseult is being courted by another favourite of Mark's, Canados. However, she repulses the latter's advances, and when Tristram arrives their former relations are resumed, and Ganhardin is betrothed to Brangwain. Canados discovers them, and they have to flee in different directions. Ganhardin returns to Brittany, Iseult to the court. Tristram disguises himself as a beggar again. A tournament is held, and Tristram and Ganhardin defeat Canados and kill their other enemies at court. They then retire to Brittany where their help is sought by a namesake of Tristram in a knightly adventure. At this point the manuscript ends.

There is little of the fire and splendour associated with the story today in this writer's telling of it. The complicated metre and rhyme seem to have taken up most of his time, leaving him little to spend on the story itself. The vocabulary is repetitive, and the narrative becomes tedious. One has only to compare *Sir Gawain and the Green Knight* at any point with this, and the depths to which even the more educated of the romance writers could sink will be realized. Nor does it possess the primitive vigour of some of the Gawain ballads. Characterization is pallid, a fault less excusable in this than in any other story.

Its moral attitude must also be condemned. It neither puts forward chivalric love as a code of honour sufficient unto itself, nor does it propound any other Christian or moral ideal, but merely condones every action of the lovers without any particular reason or excuse being offered; even the fatalistic atmosphere is absent.

Such a brief treatment does not do justice to the inherent merits of the Tristram and Iseult story, but no English work of real power and originality on this theme was to appear for close on seven hundred years after its first telling. Neither is there any great romance of this period with Lancelot as its protagonist; but this gap was soon to be remedied by Malory. Part of the reason for this was that Lancelot, associated as he was with the *amour courtois* was a very much less attractive figure for English audiences than Sir Gawain. We have only one poem in which he is the central figure, an unfinished Scottish work of the third quarter of the fifteenth century, *Lancelot du Laik*.[19] It is a free treatment of an incident in the *Livres de Lancelot* of the Vulgate Cycle. Unfortunately, it suffers from almost every kind of fault. The most irritating of these is the writer's habit of quoting things which he might tell us about, but which he must leave for the moment. He is evidently very confident of his talent, and tends to adopt a tone of familiar condescension which usually turns into mere garrulousness. He attempts unsuccessfully to imitate Chaucer in the prologue. The work as a whole is dull and trivial; the free handling of the theme, which entirely alters the relationship between Lancelot and Guinevere in which the great interest of the story lies, requires a great poet to justify it. It will be more appropriate to examine the Lancelot theme in connection with Malory.

However, the only Middle English version of the final stages of the tragedy of Arthur, does contain a reasonable treatment of the Lancelot-Guinevere theme. It dates from the last decade of the fourteenth century, and is 3,884 verses in length, in rhyming stanzas, with some alliteration. For convenience of reference it is known as the stanzaic or Harleian *Le Mort Arthur*[19] to distinguish it from the totally different chronicle-romance, the alliterative or Thornton *Morte Arthure*, which we have already discussed.

The romance opens four years after the quest of the Holy Grail has been achieved. A tournament is to be held at Winchester, which Lancelot wishes to attend in disguise. He counterfeits old age as he rides along unfrequented roads on his way there, but just as he is passing the castle at which Arthur and Ywain are staying, his horse stumbles, and he betrays himself by his agility and horsemanship in not falling. They, however, allow him to continue on his way without greeting him. He stays the night at the castle of Ascalot, where the lord's daughter falls violently in love with him. He will have nothing to do with her, but is forced to promise to wear her token at the tournament by way of conciliation. Her brother accompanies him, and, wearing plain armour, with a token on his crest, he is victorious in the lists. The knights of Arthur's court, who naturally recognized him from his feats of arms, are baffled by the token, which Lancelot would never normally have worn. However, although he defeats all comers, he is severely wounded in the last combat, so that when the King proclaims a second tournament a month later, in order to discover the stranger's identity, he is unable to attend. He is cared for by the lady of Ascalot, and has to leave his armour with her as a pledge of a speedy return when he departs. Unfortunately, Gawain happens to discover this, and Guinevere, when told, grows violently jealous. On Lancelot's arrival, she reproves him strongly, whereupon he departs again precipitously, unable to understand the reason for this outburst.

Soon afterwards a distinguished Scottish knight dies after eating an apple given to him by the Queen. The squire who had poisoned it had intended that Gawain should receive it, but as a result the Queen is accused by the dead knight's brother of having caused his death. Arthur has to sanction a single combat to decide the question, but Guinevere cannot find a champion. Fortunately Lancelot hears of the affair and prepares for battle. Meanwhile, the lady of Ascalot has died of grief, and her body is floated down the river to Camelot, in accordance with her last wishes. The barge is brought to shore by Arthur's orders, and a letter of explanation makes Gawain and Guinevere realize their mistake. Lancelot appears in the nick of time, and overcomes the knight's brother. The Queen forgives him, Arthur presents him with Joyous Gard castle, and all seems to be well.

Agravaine, Gawain's brother, and Mordred, Arthur's son, have, however, decided to accuse the two lovers openly, in spite of Gawain's warnings. Arthur has to consent to a trap being laid for them. He is to go hunting, leaving them alone at the castle and Mordred, Agravaine and ten other knights are to surprise them together. All goes as expected; but Lancelot has been warned, and, although he refuses to take armour, has a sword

with him. He kills the first knight who appears, and holds the
door shut while he puts on his armour. He then disposes of all
except Mordred, who escapes. He is forced to flee to the forest,
and Guinevere is condemned to the stake in his absence, much
to the dismay of Gawain and his two brothers, Gareth and
Gaheris. These two attend the burning unarmed, and when
Lancelot cuts his way through the mob to rescue Guinevere,
they are accidently killed.

Gawain swears to avenge the death of his brothers, and joins
the army which Arthur has fitted out in order to besiege Joyous
Gard, where Lancelot and Guinevere have taken refuge. After a
protracted siege, the Pope compels both sides to declare a truce.
Guinevere has to return to Arthur, but Lancelot is forced by the
King and Gawain to return to his native Brittany. Mordred is
appointed regent, and Arthur pursues the war on the other side
of the Channel. Lancelot is once more besieged; and a series of
single combats between the champions of the two sides ensue,
culminating in one in which Lancelot severely wounds Gawain,
but spares his life. Gawain renews the challenge when he has
recovered, but is again defeated and spared.

News of Mordred's treachery now reaches Arthur, and he has
to return in all haste to Britain. Mordred has had himself
crowned, and attempted to wed Guinevere, who has shut herself up in the Tower of London. He has to discontinue his siege
to repel his father's landing. Arthur is successful, although
Gawain is killed in the struggle. After a foreboding dream he
decides to postpone further battle with Mordred, and to seek a
truce. Parleys begin, but a knight draws his sword to kill an
adder, and, both sides having independently agreed that this
shall be the signal to attack if necessary, battle is joined. At the
end of the day, only Arthur, Mordred, and two other knights are
left alive. Arthur kills Mordred, but is severely wounded himself. He commands Bedivere to throw his sword Excalibur into
the sea. Bedivere hesitates, but finally does so. Arthur is borne
away to Avalon. Bedivere wanders through the forest and comes

at daybreak to a chapel, where he finds the Archbishop of Canterbury kneeling at a sumptuous newly-made tomb, which had appeared mysteriously during the previous night. He discovers that here lies Arthur, and joins the Archbishop in his devotions.

Lancelot, accompanied by Bors and Lionel, now arrives in Britain, and seeing that he is too late to help Arthur, goes in search of the Queen. He finds her in a convent: but she tells him that she has resolved to become a nun, and he decides to become a hermit. He comes by chance to Bedivere's chapel, and is, after seven years, ordained priest there. Shortly afterwards he dies; and Guinevere, who only survives him by a few days, is buried in the same chapel, next to Arthur.

This is a fairly straightforward reproduction of the Vulgate Cycle, *La Mort Artu*. The immediate original of the first part is lost; there are minor variations from known texts of the French up to v. 1,672.[21] *La Mort Artu* presented better material for translation than many other works chosen, and hence this romance is one of the more successful transfers. An admirable dramatic flow, due to a concise and rapid style, with a direct and simple vocabulary and imagery, made this poem better suited to the tastes of the English audience than for example, *Ywain and Gawain*. This audience was neither the yeomen for whom the ballads and cruder poems were produced, nor was it the equivalent of the courtly circles to whom the French poets were accustomed to address their works; it was rather the merchant and knight, such as the fellow-member of the Skinner's Company, for whom, at a later date, Henry Lovelich was to make his translations. Hence rather more of the love element is retained than might otherwise have been the case, but this remains subordinate to the main action.

Here Lancelot has replaced Gawain as first knight of Arthur's court. It is his amours with Guinevere and the consequences of them that occupy the early part of the book. The incident of Lancelot and the Fair Maid of Ascalot, who dies of unrequited love for him, appears in English for the first time, nor is its telling

entirely unworthy of the superb versions of Malory and Tennyson, which were to follow. Mordred's treachery and the final
battles are little altered from the chronicles, the 'Fortune's
Wheel' dream being included. The poem concludes, however,
with Lancelot's death, as in Malory, but the writer fails to make
full use of the human tragedy of the situation, becoming merely
insipid at the point where the highest pathos should have been
reached. As a whole, nonetheless, the poem is successful.

The remaining two Middle English Arthurian romances are
outside the framework of the main story. *Sir Libeaus Desconus*[22]
is again a near-direct translation from a late French romance,
the source of Renart de Beaujeu's work of the same name. The
English translation has been attributed to Thomas Chestre,
author of *Launfal*, but this seems unlikely, as the style is considerably different. It was one of the more popular romances,
and we possess six manuscripts of it. It appears to have been
written in south-east England about the middle of the fourteenth
century, and is 2,232 verses in length.

Gyngalyn, Gawain's son, is brought up by his mother in the
depths of a forest: she gives him no other name than 'fair son',
and he never asks what his true name may be. One day he finds a
dead knight in the forest where he is hunting deer, and takes his
armour. He goes to Arthur's court, and the king asks him his
name. As he cannot reply anything other than 'fair son', the
king decrees that he shall be known as the Fair Unknown—
Libeaus Desconus. He is trained in the knightly arts by Gawain,
who does not recognize his son. When he is knighted, he begs to
be allowed to undertake the first adventure that is offered to
one of Arthur's knights.

A maiden, Elene by name, comes to ask assistance for her lady,
who is in the power of two enchanters. She scorns Libeaus Desconus as being too inexperienced for the adventure, but Arthur
will not send anyone else, and she reluctantly departs with him.
He overthrows the first knight to challenge him, and makes him
go to Arthur's court to do homage. The three nephews of this

knight attempt to kill him, but Libeaus defeats them and sends them likewise to Arthur. He then encounters two giants, who are successively slain, and Elene acknowledges his valour. He meets her father, who gives him various presents, and continues on his way. As they approach a castle, the maiden tells him of the custom observed there: that any knight who can find a lady fairer than the mistress of the castle is given a gerfalcon by its lord, Sir Giffroun: but if the challenger's lady is the less beautiful of the two, he must fight with Sir Giffroun. Libeaus takes up the challenge, in spite of the maiden's warning that Sir Giffroun is an enchanter. As expected, Elene is no match for the lady, but Libeaus overthrows the knight. Word of this reaches Arthur, and he sends Libeaus a hundred pounds, with which he holds a great feast at Giffroun's castle.

He then proceeds on his way, and after an incident over a brachet* which Elene takes a fancy to, and in connection with which he defeats a dozen knights single-handed, he comes to the Ile d'Or, which is being besieged by a gigantic black man named Maugirs. He defeats the latter, in spite of a treacherous blow which makes him fall into a stream from which he is drinking during a temporary truce. The lady of the castle bewitches Libeaus, and he falls in love with her. He remains there a year, until Elene reminds him one day that his original errand, the rescue of the lady of Sinadoun, remains unaccomplished. He departs at once with the lady's steward as his squire, and at last reaches Sinadoun. He gains entrance after defeating the constable of the castle, who tells him that the lady is held prisoner by two magicians, Mabon and Yrain, whereupon he goes alone to the palace in the centre of the castle. It is very richly built, but empty save for musicians. He sits down on a chair on the dais at the end of the Great Hall, and the musicians vanish, the whole building shakes, and the magicians enter, equipped to fight him. He kills Mabon, but Yrain vanishes before he can despatch him. Startled, he prays for protection against sorcery. However, Yrain does not

* A small dog, often a lady's lapdog.

intervene again; but a serpent with a woman's face appears and kisses him before he can prevent her. As soon as this happens, the serpent becomes the lady of Sinadoun, who says that all is well now that she has kissed a knight of Gawain's kin. Libeaus returns with her to Arthur's court, where they are married.

The great appeal of *Sir Libeaus Desconus* stems from its content rather than any poetic merit. It is virtually a compendium of every type of Arthurian adventure with some magic added. To enumerate the details of its sources would be a lengthy matter. But there is little in it that has not been traced back to Celtic folklore.[23] The final adventure by which the lady of Sinadoun is disenchanted is known as the 'Fier Baiser' (Proud Kiss), and is always attached to a son of Gawain. The scornful companion is found again in Malory in the shape of Lyonet, whose adventures with Gareth are a simplified version of the present story.[24]

In style and literary qualities the work is not outstanding. It relies, as we have observed, on incident rather than analysis and observation for its interest, and achieves its object satisfactorily. But it never rises above the mediocre in this respect. This is the opposite extreme in subject-matter to Chrétien's works: the latter subordinates plot to character, whereas here the plot is all-important.

The last romance proper we have to discuss is *Launfal* by Thomas Chestre,[25] of similar period to the preceding poem, but only half as long.

At Guinevere's wedding to Arthur, Launfal, who has protested against Arthur's choice of bride because of her lascivious reputation, is the only one who does not receive a gift. He departs from the wedding feast with two other knights on a pretext, and returns to Caerleon, his native city. He wishes to stay at the mayor's house, the mayor being an old friend, but the latter on hearing of his quarrel with Arthur tries to turn him away; however, he finally relents, and Launfal stays there for a year, at the end of which time he is reduced to such poverty that his two companions ask leave of him to return to Arthur's court, which he readily grants them, on condition that they tell no one of his estate. They keep their promise; the Queen, who naturally dislikes Launfal, is angry when she hears that all is well with him. Meanwhile, he is in fact in such straits that he cannot even go to Mass, as his clothes are so ragged. He borrows a horse and rides disconsolately out of Caerleon. Soon he reaches a forest, and rests at midday in the shade of a tree. Two maidens approach and say that their lady, Triamour, wishes to speak with him. He follows them, and falls in love with Triamour as soon as he sees her. She tells him that she has learnt of his plight, and has long loved him. She offers wonderful gifts if he will be her lover. There is only one condition—he must never speak of her. He readily agrees. The next morning, he returns to Caerleon and is met by a train of servants bearing her gifts, among whom is Geoffrey, who becomes his squire. He gives a feast for fifty of the poor, and a tournament is held in which he is victorious. Triamour visits him every night, unknown to all save him and Geoffrey.

Valentine, a knight of Lombardy, grows jealous of Launfal's fame and challenges him to a combat. Launfal, with Geoffrey's timely assistance, kills him at the third joust and escapes. Arthur, hearing of this, invites Launfal to a feast in his honour. Here the Queen makes advances to him, which he scornfully rejects. In doing so he boasts of Triamour, and says that the lowliest maid of her train is fairer than the queen. Immediately his possessions and attendants vanish, and he is cast into prison for insulting the Queen, who promises to let herself be blinded if Launfal can show he speaks the truth. Launfal is commanded to produce his lady within a year and a fortnight, but cannot do so. But the knights appointed to judge him refuse to condemn him. Just as Guinevere is trying to persuade Arthur to have him killed, Triamour appears, rescues Launfal, and, in accordance with her oath, blinds the queen. Launfal vanishes with her to the isle of Oleroun.

The French lai from which the story is taken, *Lanval*, attributed to Marie de France, is definitely Celtic in origin, the atmosphere of faery throughout being a common feature of Celtic folk-tales, as is the fairy mistress theme itself.[26] Thomas Chestre has made two interpolations: the tournament at Caerleon and the fight with Valentine. This was probably a concession to the popular taste for military episodes; the latter incident is probably borrowed from another of Marie de France's lais, *Graelent*. The Arthurian setting which has been grafted on to this older stock has the characteristics of a late stage of development. Guinevere's character may, however, represent the Welsh view of her, as in the *Awntyrrs of Arthur*, that of a lascivious and unfaithful queen; for once she is appropriately punished.

We have a similar version of the same work under the title *Landeval*, in the southern dialect, dating from the following century. It does not appear to be an abbreviation of the previous work, but a fresh translation. It omits the interpolated parts, and is just over half the length of *Launfal*. It is more effective for this, since it gains in unity.

So far, there have been no masterpieces in our survey; but neither have there been any really crude works. Even the more mediocre efforts show some attempt at literary polish. But, when we turn to the most popular hero of the English medieval writers, Gawain, we find both extremes: a great work of art, and pieces which have no interest whatsoever as literature. It is here that the range of Arthurian literature may best be judged.

SIX

GAWAIN

ONE knight above all others at Arthur's court fired the English poets' imagination in the Middle Ages—Gawain. This is witnessed by the relatively large number of romances in which he is the central figure, and by the fact that he is always held up as the epitome of knighthood. In the early French romances, he is indeed of great knightly skill, but he is also lascivious, and not always courteous. To the English, he represents the flower of all courtesy and gentleness and the figure of every virtue; the other knights, with the one exception of Arthur, are usually foils to his prowess and nobility.

Gawain first appears in Geoffrey of Monmouth's *Historia Regum Britanniae*, where he is called Walgainus. He resembles the Gwalchmai of Welsh legend and Cuchullinn in the Irish epics. Like the latter, he possesses many of the properties of a sun-hero, such as the increase of his strength until midday and its decline thereafter. He was the real owner of Excalibur, which was originally a dazzling sun-weapon. Of all the knights of the Round Table, he has the longest connection with Arthur, save for Kay and Bedivere, appearing as Arthur's nephew in Geoffrey of Monmouth's work. Like Cuchullinn, he is a folk-tale hero, and hence is the central figure in primitive stories rather than artificial literature.

Yet the first of the poems of which he is hero, *Sir Gawain and the Green Knight*,[1] is the most superb accomplishment of this artificial literature, the only great Middle English Arthurian work, and one of the great masterpieces of the poetry of this period as a whole, both in its treatment of the subject-matter and in the strength of its style and imagery, which represents the climax of English alliterative poetry. The unique manuscript[2] contains in addition three other poems of the same period, by the same writer; all are in West Midland dialect with a strong Scandinavian influence, which is at its most marked in *Sir Gawain and the Green Knight*. This seems to have been the earliest of the four, written between 1370 and 1390. One critic believes it to have been commissioned by John of Gaunt,[3] and there is strong evidence for the connection, if not for the actual commission. The identity of the unknown genius has long been a matter for debate. No suggestion yet put forward has gained more than a handful of supporters, and as usual in such cases attempts have been made to find internal evidence in the shape of puns, and even numerological evidence,[4] which will reveal the identity of its author. All that can be said with certainty about the writer is that he was well acquainted with courtly life, could read Latin and French, and was probably a scholar of some merit. He might well have been, or have become, as the tone of his later poems suggests, a clerk in minor orders.

The poem opens with an account of the founding of Britain, and tells us that Arthur was the greatest and most honoured of Britain's kings. The story proper then begins. Arthur is at Camelot one Christmastide, and on New Year's Day, in accordance with his custom, does not eat until some adventure has taken place. Soon a gigantic knight appears, entirely clad in green, and riding a green horse. He demands to see Arthur, who asks him what he wants. The knight has a bargain to propose: any of Arthur's knights who is bold enough to strike off his head with the axe he has brought, may do so, provided that he accepts a return blow in a year's time. None of the knights comes forward, and the Green Knight taunts them with cowardice. Arthur

angrily leaps forward to take up the challenge himself, but
Gawain restrains him, and asks permission to undertake the
adventure himself. Arthur grants it, and Gawain beheads the
Green Knight. To the astonishment of all, the latter picks up
his head, which admonishes Gawain to meet him at the Green
Chapel in a year's time, and gallops away with it under his arm.

Next All-Hallows day, Gawain is armed in preparation for his
departure in search of the mysterious trysting-place. He rides
through the kingdom of Logres to North Wales, and eventually
reaches the wilderness of Wirral, by way of Anglesey, Holyhead
and the coast. By now it is Christmas, and he finds himself in a
vast, dreary forest. He kneels down and prays, and shortly afterwards comes to a splendid castle, where he finds the desired shel-
ter for the night, and learns that the Green Chapel is but a few
miles away. The lord of the castle invites him to remain until the
New Year, which is in three days' time. He also proposes a bargain; he will go hunting on these three days, and Gawain shall
remain at the castle with his wife. At the end of each day they
will exchange their spoils.

The hunts take place with due ceremony; and meanwhile the
lady visits Gawain each morning while is is still lying in bed and
tempts him to be unchaste with her in her lord's absence. He,
however, turns aside her advances with courteous but artful
speeches. At the end of each day, Gawain and the lord duly exchange their day's winnings: Gawain gives one kiss for several
deer on the first day, and two kisses for a boar on the second.
However, on the third day, the lady gives him a magical green
lace girdle which protects the wearer from all harm, and three
kisses as well; but Gawain keeps this and gives the lord only the
three kisses, for which he receives a fox's skin. He has thus
broken the agreement.

Early next morning, Gawain makes his way to the Green
Chapel with one of the lord's servants, who warns him of the
fearful strength of the Green Knight and advises him to turn
back. Gawain refuses, but, finding the Green Chapel deserted,

H

is about to go, when he hears the sound of an axe being whetted,
and discovers the Green Knight preparing for the encounter.
Gawain bows to receive the blow, but the Green Knight accuses
him of flinching when he lifts the axe. He promises to keep still,
and the Green Knight lifts the axe again, but lowers it without
striking. Finally he lifts it again and lets it fall in such a way that
it slightly grazes Gawain's neck. He then reveals that he is the
lord of the castle at which Gawain had stayed, and that his wife
had tempted Gawain in accordance with his instructions. The
two feints were in payment for the kisses, and the graze was for
the magic lace which he had kept against the terms of the bargain.
Gawain is ashamed at being found out, and offers to give
back the lace, but is made to keep it and wear it in memory of his
disgrace. The Green Knight tells him that his name is Bernlak
de Hautdesert, and that it was Morgan le Fay who had arranged
the adventure in order to prove the Round Table and to frighten
Guinevere. Gawain returns to Arthur's court, and, although
much embarrassed, relates his adventures. The king decrees that
all knights of the Round Table shall wear a green baldric in
memory of the adventure.

In this tale there are two distinct parts which have been skilfully welded into one. The Green Knight's challenge to Gawain
is an example of a Celtic episode that we may call the Beheading
Game. The approaches of the hostess at the castle, are the other
part, the Temptation. Both incidents are of great age and have a
long pedigree. In the case of the Beheading Game, the earliest
form of the story is to be found in the Irish epic *Fled Bricrend*
(Bricreu's Feast), in which it is part of the contest for the cham-
pionship of Ulster, with Cuchullinn as its hero. Even here it
occurs twice in variant forms, and must have come from an
earlier recited version of about the eighth century, for the tale is
considerably older than the written form, and the manuscript
dates from the tenth century. From Ireland it passed to France,
possibly via Wales and Brittany, and by comparing the details of
the stories in which it is found, we can reconstruct the original

LITERARY DESCENT OF *SIR GAWAIN AND THE GREEN KNIGHT*

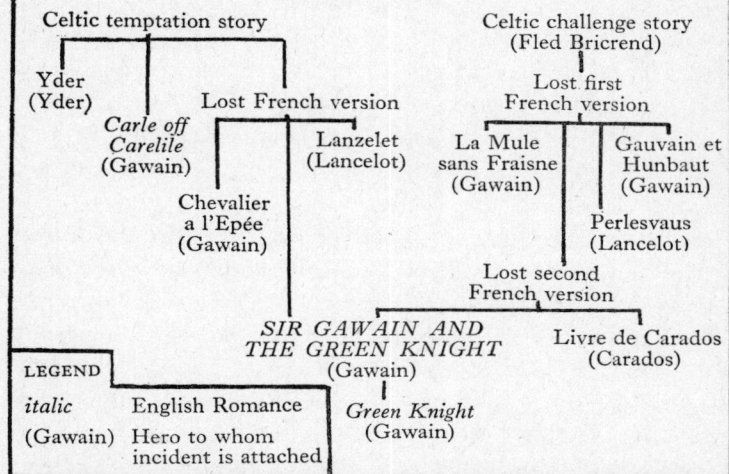

Celtic temptation story

Yder
(Yder)

Carle off Carelile
(Gawain)

Lost French version

Chevalier
a l'Epée
(Gawain)

Lanzelet
(Lancelot)

Celtic challenge story
(Fled Bricrend)

Lost first
French version

La Mule
sans Fraisne
(Gawain)

Gauvain et
Hunbaut
(Gawain)

Perlesvaus
(Lancelot)

Lost second
French version

SIR GAWAIN AND THE GREEN KNIGHT
(Gawain)

Livre de Carados
(Carados)

Green Knight
(Gawain)

LEGEND

italic — English Romance
(Gawain) — Hero to whom incident is attached

COMPARISON OF DETAILS OF VARIOUS VERSIONS

	I	C	G	O	R	M	P	H
1	Black giant	Green attire tall knight	Green attire	Churl	Churl	Churl	Tall knight	Churl
2	Axe	Long sword	Axe	Axe	Axe	Axe	Axe	Axe
3	Challenge threat	Challenge *jeu parti*	Challenge *jeu parti*	Challenge threat	Challenge *jeu parti*	Challenge threat	Challenge threat	Challenge threat
4	Taunts	Taunts	Taunts	Taunts	Taunts			
5	Feints	Feints	Feints	Feints	Feints		Feints	
6	Harmless blow	Harmless blow	Graze	Harmless blow	Harmless blow	No actual blow	No final blow	

Key:
I—Irish *Fled Bricrend* (first version).
C—*Livre de Carados*.
G—*Sir Gawain and the Green Knight*.
O—First lost French version.
R—Second lost French version.
M—*La Mule sans Fraisne*.
P—*Perlesvaus*.
H—*Hunbaut*.

1. Character and description of challenger.
2. Weapon used.
3. Type of challenge:
jeu parti: challenger to receive first stroke and to return it within a stated time.
threat: if challenged does not behead challenger, latter will give first blow.
4. When no one comes forward, challenger taunts the assembled company with cowardice.
5. When the challenger returns the blow, he makes one or more feints.
6. The nature of the blow received by the challenged.

translation. Three French romances made use of this; in two cases Gawain is the hero, in the other, it is Lancelot. A second version must have been made, for the Beheading Game is found in the *Livre de Carados* in a rather different form which is nearer to that in *Sir Gawain and the Green Knight*. The basic elements in all cases are a supernatural being who is beheaded without apparent harm and who returns his half of the bargain with a harmless blow.[5]

The Temptation story is similarly Celtic in origin, the nearest parallel being found in *Pwyll*, one of the stories in the Welsh *Mabinogi*. This presents three major points of resemblance: the noble huntsman introduces the hero as a guest, a temptation scene in which the huntsman's wife is rejected by the hero, and, more incidental, a year's interval between a related challenge incident and its sequel. The huntsman is also the same colour as his horse, in this case grey; in the English poem both are green.[6] We have also two French stories from a similar original; the first, in the romance *Yder*, differs considerably from the other group, for here the hero repulses the temptress physically and handles her roughly. This probably represents one of two Irish versions; the other is the source of the incident in *Sir Gawain and the Carl of Carlisle*, in which the host puts Gawain into his wife's bed, orders him to kiss her three times, but forbids him to go further. In reward for his obedience he is given the host's daughter. This, however, belongs to the group of Imperious Host stories in which obedience is the crucial factor. The other French parallel, in the *Chevalier à l'Epée*, is confused by the introduction of other features such as the Enchanted Bed, which kills anyone who sleeps in it. A third person, in the German *Lanzelet*, has a temptress acting of her own free will whose advances are accepted. We possess no clear-cut line of descent here as in the case of the Beheading Game, but there seems to have been a French story of this type current which was used by the poet of *Sir Gawain and the Green Knight*.

When these two stories, the Beheading Game and Temptation,

were combined, has long been disputed. One school of thought
favours a lost French original containing both; the other argues
that a poet of the stature of the author of *Sir Gawain and the
Green Knight* would be perfectly capable of making such a fusion.
Let us for the moment accept the latter view; but fortunately
the poem's merit is in no way dependent on it. Whoever did
make the two stories one was a brilliant sculptor of poetic form;
for the outcome of one half is made to depend on the other with
extreme subtlety. The crux is the exchange of spoils during the
three days' hunting, which provides a motive for the slight blow
given to Gawain by the Green Knight, for he has broken the
agreement by concealing the green lace instead of giving it in
exchange for the fox's skin. Thus, while the Temptation arose
naturally enough out of the Challenge, yet this addition makes
the issue of the Challenge depend on the outcome of the Temptation. But such subtlety of plot must be matched by the verse
and language if the poem is to succeed. And here at last is a poet
writing an Arthurian romance who is capable of the task. The
alliterative verse in his hands is a tool adapted to any purpose he
cares to turn it to. Everything descriptive is material for a small
masterpiece; the loving portrayal of the Green Knight's axe

> 'A spetos sparthe to expoun   in spelle who might'
> The hede of an elnyarde   the large lenkthe hade,
> The grain al of grene stele   and of golde hewen,
> The bit burnist bright   with a brode edge
> As wel shapen to schere   as sharp rasores.
> The stele of a stif staf   the sturne hit bi gripte
> That was wounden with iron   to the wandes ende,
> And al bigraven with grene   in gravios werkes.*

and of the arming of Gawain before he departs on his quest for

---

* 'Let he who will set forth in verse the fine points of a battle-axe';
The head was a full yard in length, the sides of green steel decorated
with gold; the edge was burnished and broad, as well shaped for cutting as sharp rasors. The shaft was a strong staff, its handle bound with
iron to the foot, and skilfully engraved in green . . .

the Green Chapel, are but two examples. But the greatest passages are those in which the poet depicts Nature and her ways. The two verses at the opening of the second part describe the changing seasons between Christmas and Michaelmas; they alone surpass all conventional attempts at such poetry. But they are followed by the harsh weather that Gawain encounters on his northward journey, where in the sound of the words and the rugged rhythms is captured the very spirit of winter. The northern countryside in which the poet lived rises up before us in its most severe and impressive beauty. Across this background sweep past the three days' hunting; and few poets have caught the atmosphere of the chase so exactly; days of exhilaration, danger, triumph, and noble ritual, and at the end of each a homecoming to a warm welcome and a blazing fire when the last horn has been blown. On the day of the tryst at the Green Chapel, the countryside seems grim once more; the hills are mist-mantled, there is hoar frost in the oakwoods, snow in the valleys. But possibly the finest picture of all is that of Gawain lying awake on New Year's Day, waiting for dawn and listening to the gale outside:

> 'Now neghes the New Yere   and the night passes,
> The day drives to the derk   as Drighten biddes;
> Bot wilde wederes of the worlde   wakned theroute,
> Cloudes kesten kenly   the colde to the erthe,
> With nighe innoghe of the northe,   the naked to tene;
> The snawe snitered ful snart,   that snayped the wilde;
> The werbelande winde   wapped fro the highe,
> And drof eche dale ful   of driftes ful grete.
> The leude listened ful wel   that ley in his bedde,
> Thagh he lowkes his liddes,   ful littel he slepes;
> Bi ech kok that crue   he knew wel the steven.'*

* Now the New Year draws near, and the night passes; drives daylight off darkness, as our Lord ordained. But the world outside was full of wild weather; the clouds cast bitter cold on the earth that came from the north and caused the flesh pain; the snow fell bleakly, and froze the

The people of this harsh, real world are equally alive; their feasts and merrymaking, gaiety and good cheer are far from the delicate but artificial world of the French romances, and their conversations are as unforced and natural as those of the heroes and heroines of Chrétien de Troyes are studied and literary.

Only one character seems contradictory: the Green Knight himself. In the beheading incidents he is a superhuman being with strange powers, who moves in an aura of mystery. But in the Temptation, he becomes the gay, friendly lord of a rich castle. The poet in combining the two stories was unable to find a suitable equation between the two characters, and had to make the Green Knight a shape-shifter. This may seem unsatisfactory to the modern reader; but the medieval mind delighted in such things. And the strange legendary world of Norse and Saxon literature is never far from the poet's mind; Gawain encounters dragons, trolls and giants on his journey northward. The fact that the magical Green Knight can also appear as an ordinary nobleman makes him all the more striking.

Finally, the skill of the poet in handling verse and language is not wasted on a mere romance. The English poet has given his story a definite moral and didactic tone. Gawain, the model of knighthood, only escapes the fatal return blow because he holds out against the lady's adulterous temptations. This is a far cry from the French writers' easy acceptance, in fact exaltation, of *amour courtois*. They would probably have admired such a sin, even though it contravened the strictest conception of this code. Yet they would have agreed with his punishment, for by breaking his word in concealing the lace, he has dishonoured the order of knighthood. The English poet, however, has a far higher idea of the latter, too; we find several religious features in the work, especially in the Pentangle device borne by Gawain on his shield,[7] and in the several references to him as 'Mary's knight'. There is

wild beasts; the whirling wind wailed from the heights, and filled each valley with great drifts. The knight (i.e. Gawain) listened as he lay in bed; though his eyes were closed, he slept but little, and knew the hour from the cock's crowing.

an idealism throughout that raises the poem far above the level of the other English romances, and reminds one of Wolfram von Eschenbach. Gawain is an idealized hero who makes one error that cannot be redeemed, although not fatal; Parzival, on the other hand, although he almost fails in the Grail quest when he does not ask the required question the first time, gains a second opportunity by long years of atonement. The common subject of Wolfram and the Gawain-poet is the search for perfection, typified in the former by the achievement of the Grail, and in the other by the preservation of knightly honour in face of temptation. And the Gawain-poet is more pessimistic than Wolfram, for the latter regards perfection as eventually attainable, while he sees any striving towards it as inevitably doomed to failure but not to disaster. Some writers have seen *Gawain and the Green Knight* as a poem with a didactic moral; but it is rather a moral reflection on human weakness.

In *Sir Gawain and the Green Knight* the Arthurian legend leaves its realms of isolated fantasy to become natural and human; and new splendour of a far more enduring kind is the result. Language, style and a subtle framework combine into a superb achievement beside which every other English medieval poem on Arthur pales into literary insignificance; and nowhere else does the tradition of the romances produce such a high idealism and sustained exaltation of chivalry.

The condensed and corrupt ballad form of this masterpiece, *The Greene Knight*,[8] is completely unworthy of its great original. Its vocabulary and style mark the lowest ebb of the fifteenth-century ballads. The plot is maltreated, and its motive becomes the improbable love of the lady of the castle for Gawain, whom she has never seen. This betrays a straightforward approach far removed from the attitude of the earlier romance writers, a concern with cause and effect which is alien to the material. The result of this change is to divest the completion of the Challenge of its real importance, a process continued by the alteration of

Gawain's bargain with the host. There is only one day's hunting
and they agree to share the spoils. Since the lace cannot be
shared, Gawain's guilt is considerably lessened.

Throughout the poem, the subtler shades of meaning and implication are bluntly stated by the later writer. The only interest
this crude production can have for us is to emphasize by contrast the great heights and depths of which English romances on
Arthur were capable. Here are two parallel passages from the
poems; they describe Gawain's journey to the Green Chapel
where he is to meet the challenger. Firstly, *The Greene Knight*:

> 'When he rode over the mold,
> His geere glistered as gold,
>   By the way as he rode;
> Many furleys there saw he,
> Fowles by the water did flee,
>   By brimes and bankes soe broad.
>
> Many furleys there saw he,
> Of wolves and wild beasts sikerlye,
>   On hunting he tooke most heede;
> Forth he rode, the sooth to tell,
> For to seeke the Greene Chappell,
>   He wist not where indeed.'*

Now the account given by the poet of *Sir Gawain and the Green
Knight*:

> 'Mony clif he overclambe in contrayes straunge,
> Fer floten fro his frendes fremedly he rides.
> At eche warthe other water ther the wighe passed
> He fonde a foo him before, bot ferly hit were,
> And that so foule and so felle that feght him behode.

* When he rode through the countryside, his armour glistered like
gold, as he rode on his way. He saw many wonders there; birds fled
across the water, by lakes and banks so broad. He saw many wonders
there, of wolves and wild beasts, and paid much attention to hunting; in
truth, he rode out to seek the Green Chapel, and he had no idea where
it was.

So mony mervayl bi mount　ther the mon findes,
Hit were to tore for to telle　of the tenthe dole.
Sumwhile with wormes he werres,　and with wolves als,
Sumwhile with wodwos,　that woned in the knarres,
Bothe with bulles and bears and bores otherwhile
And etaines, that him anelede　of the heghe felle;
Nade he ben dughty and drighe,　and Drighten had served,
Douteless he hade ben ded　and dreped ful ofte.
For werre wrathed him not so much,　that winter was wors,
When the colde cler water　fro the cloudes shadde,
And fres er hit falle might　to the fale erthe;
Ner slain with the slete　he sleped in his yrnes
Mo nightes then innoghe　in naked rokkes,
Ther as claterande fro the crest　the colde borne rennes,
And henged heghe over his hede in hard iise-ikkles,
Thus in peril and paine　and plites ful harde
Bi contray cayres this knight,　til Kristmasse even,

al one;
The knight wel that tide
To Mary made his mone,
That ho wim red to ride
And wisse him to sum wone.'*

---

* He scaled many a cliff in strange country, riding far from his friends, forsaken. At every ford or stream that he passed he found a foe before him, save by some strange chance; and they were so foul and strange, yet he had to fight them. So many marvels did he meet in the mountains that it would be tedious to recount them. He fought with serpents and wolves too, sometimes with satyrs that dwelt in the rocks, with bulls and bears, and boars on other occasions, with giants that attacked him on the moors; if he had not been doughty and strong and served Our Lord, he would certainly have died and often defeated. For it was not the fights that troubled him; the wintry weather was worse, when the cold clear water fell from the clouds and froze before it could fall to the pale earth. Almost dead from the sleet he slept in his armour, night after night, among the bare rocks, where cold streams ran clattering down from the peaks, and hung over his head in bare icicles. Thus in danger and difficulty, and in many a woe, this knight travelled alone through the country until Christmas Eve. And then he complained to the Virgin and begged her to guide him until he came to some dwelling.

The beheading incident which is the main episode of *Sir Gawain and the Green Knight* recurs in several poems with the same hero, albeit in various forms. The first of them, *The Turk and Gawain*,[9] was in its earliest form* an adaptation of a Celtic folk-tale, either Irish or possibly Manx in origin. It was about 700 lines in length. In it an enchanted knight, this time in the form of a dwarf or 'turk' issues a challenge to Gawain in order to get him to undertake the adventures necessary to qualify him to perform the beheading which will break the spell. The adventures include several which have Irish parallels,[10] and these with the association with the Isle of Man, imply that the transfer has been direct from their source without a French intermediate version. It may well be an Arthurian adaptation of a 'fairy tale' from Ireland by some northern poet.

The background and general description is limited to the barest minimum; it does not involve more detail than is absolutely necessary to the plot, in which the whole interest of the story lies. The introduction is even more perfunctory than usual, and there is only one other figure, Sir Kay, 'that crabbed knight', in his normal role of foil to Gawain.

Sir Gawain and the Carl of Carlisle embodies a similar test and disenchantment story.[11] It exists in two versions: that in the Porkington manuscript of the fifteenth century, and the much corrupted poem in the Percy folio, in a different metre. The former is the earlier, although the omission of the beheading and its disenchanting effect would at first imply a later recension. However, a point so far overlooked will explain this. Where the Percy MS. inserts the decapitation, there is apparently a missing leaf in the other version, since after line 515, a new leaf is started, on which the first line is by a second but coeval hand. This implies that the leaf was lost at a very early date, and the added line was inserted to supply the rhyme.

The story is not without some interest; it is a good example of

---

* There exists only a late and corrupt version of which about half is missing.

the material of the primitive romances. Arthur and his knights go hunting, and Bishop Baldwin, Kay and Gawain pursue a deer by themselves, and lose their way. They come to the castle of the Carl of Carlisle, of which, Baldwin tells them, it is said that no man ever stayed there and escaped with his life. None the less, they enter, and meet the Carl, a hideous giant who keeps four pets in his hall—a bear, a boar, a bull and a lion. Gawain is always courteous and obedient to his host, while the others break all the rules of good conduct. He is asked by the Carl to throw a spear at him, which he obediently does; the Carl dodges the missile, and then, leading Gawain to his wife's chamber, puts him in her bed and bids him kiss her three times, but no more. He then leads him to his daughter, with whom he spends the night. The next morning the Carl bids Gawain cut off his head, which the latter reluctantly does; whereupon the Carl changes into an ordinary man, and tells Gawain that he has been under a spell which forced him to act thus until a knight obeyed all his commands, those who failed to do so being killed by him and his 'pets'. Gawain weds the Carl's daughter and they return to court, where the Carl is made a knight of the Round Table.

This romance, in its earlier form 660 verses in length, comes from the same district as *The Turk and Gawain*. It seems to be a direct translation of some Irish or Celtic story, and there is little evidence of any French version having been used. The closest parallel yet found is the Irish *Curoi's Castle*, in which the giant has similarly four beasts, the accompanying knights fail the test, and the hero obeys an order to hurl a spear at the giant.[12] A story similar to the incident of the host's daughter is found in Norse saga, but the connection is only slight.[13]

Apart from the disenchantment, the framework of the romance is an example of the Imperious Host motif found in every European folklore. Anyone arriving at the host's castle who does not implicitly obey his word, even if politeness would seem to require disobedience, is automatically killed. This trial would be an obvious qualifying test for the disenchantment by decapitation, which can only be performed by the bravest of knights. So, in spite of wide superficial variations *The Turk and Gawain* and *Sir Gawain and the Carl of Carlisle* are in fact two forms of the same theme.

As in the other 'primitive' stories, background and description are drastically abbreviated. The writer does include, presumably to show off his knowledge of such stories, a catalogue of the knights of Arthur's court, among whom there are several of whom we know little. This apparent familiarity with romance and its setting is belied by the description of the feast at the end; his attitude is one of awe and wonder, so far as his crude technique can convey such emotions, in contrast to the casual tone of the French writers on similar occasions, who imply that these are everyday matters to them. But once again any merits the poem possesses are obscured by its rough phrasing and uneven verse.

The last poem of this group is *The Wedding of Sir Gawain and Dame Ragnell*,[14] originally 925 lines in length.* It is in the South Midland dialect of about 1450. As in so many of these poems it opens with a hunting expedition by Arthur. He parts company with the others to pursue a giant hart, and meets a knight named Sir Gromersomer Joure, who claims that his lands have been wrongfully given to Sir Gawain, and says that he will kill Arthur unless he finds out within a year what women most desire. Arthur has to promise to return, and sets about finding the required answer. He is given enough different replies to fill a large volume; but on the day before his appointment with Gromersomer Joure he meets a hideous hag who tells him that she alone knows the correct one, which she will give him on condition that she may wed Gawain. The King says that he will ask Gawain, who agrees without hesitation. The hag, by name Dame Ragnell, then informs Arthur that women most desire 'to have the sovereignty'. She will only hold him to the bargain if this is the right answer. Having tried all the other replies, Arthur finally

* A leaf is wanting in the unique MS.

gives Gromersomer Joure that of the hag, which is indeed correct. Gawain has to wed her, to the sorrow of the court, even
though he seems cheerful enough. At the wedding feast Ragnell
disgusts everyone by eating as much as six men. They retire to
bed, and Ragnell demands a kiss from her husband. It is given
and she turns into a beautiful maiden, who says that she may be
like this either by day or night, according to his choice. Gawain,
in accordance with the answer she had given Arthur earlier, puts
the matter in her hands, and as a result is told that she will always
retain her new form.

This story, of the loathly bride who must win a handsome husband in order to be freed from a spell, is one of the commonest
of folk-tales. An Irish version occurs in the twelfth-century *Book
of Ballynote*; the present version may have been Scandinavian in
origin, or have been influenced by Scandinavian tales, especially
in the detail of the bride's grotesque appetite.

Other English tellings of it are to be found in Gower's *Con-
fessio Amantis*, and in *The Wife of Bath's Tale*. The Chaucerian
version is probably the best-known of the three, but has the least
connections with Arthur. The introduction would appear to
show that Chaucer knew the story on which *The Gest of Sir
Gawain* was based; for the main story, he used, with free adaptations, an earlier version of *The Wedding of Sir Gawain*. It is the
rape of Brandelis's sister which is the central incident of *The
Gest of Sir Gawain* that causes the question: 'What do women
most desire?' Gawain is fittingly punished by having to marry
the hideous hag who provides the answer. The feast, obviously
in Chaucer's original, is omitted, with the remark that there was
no feasting on such a sad occasion. And the final choice is very
different: Gawain's bride can either remain hideous and be faithful to her husband, or he can have her beautiful and take his
chance. By giving her the choice, he gets her both beautiful and
faithful.

Both this free version, and the rather closer one of *The Wedding of Sir Gawain* come from a common original in which

Gawain was hero, since Chaucer is unlikely to have added an
Arthurian background, and yet, because of the discrepancy in
dates, cannot have used the present version of *The Wedding*.
Malory must have known either this or its predecessor, for he
mentions Sir Gromersomer Joure.*

There is little remarkable in the poem's style, which is very
much inferior to *The Wife of Bath's Tale*, although less crude
and grotesque than the other works of the 'primitive' group.
Had the Chaucerian version stronger associations with Arthurian literature, it would rank as second only to *Sir Gawain and the
Green Knight*. As it is, it hardly falls within our scope, having no
more than a name or two and half a dozen lines of introduction
to identify it with Arthur and his court.

Three other Gawain poems follow the usual pattern of translation from French originals. The first, *Ywain and Gawain*,[15] a
poem in northern dialect dating from the first half of the fourteenth century, is a direct translation of Chrétien de Troyes's
romance, *Yvain ou Le Chevalier au Lion*.[16] Certain points do,
however, suggest that the writer may have known the Welsh version in the *Mabinogion*, as for instance the description of the
beasts tended by the churl of whom Ywain enquires the way to
the fountain.†

The poem follows the French very closely in the outline. It
begins as Colgrevance is relating an adventure to his fellows outside the door of the King's bedchamber, when the Queen suddenly joins them. Taunted by Kay, and urged on by her, he continues the tale, which is not very greatly to his credit. On his
travels, he met a monstrous creature who directed him to go a
fountain in the forest of Broceliande, and there to pour some of
its water on to a rock near by. He did so, and a terrible storm
burst over him. When it subsided, a strange knight appeared,
who jousted with him and defeated him.

* Identical with Sir Grummor Grummorson.
† See J. D. Bruce, *Evolution of Arthurian Romance to 1300*, and R. S.
Loomis, *Arthurian Tradition and Chrétien de Troyes*, for argument as to
Chrétien's use of the *Mabinogion*.

Arthur comes out of his chamber, and the Queen tells him the story. He swears that he will seek this adventure, but Ywain, Colgrevance's cousin, secretly sets out before him. He reaches the fountain, where everything happens as before, except that Ywain is the victor in the ensuing combat. He pursues the knight of the fountain to his castle, which he tries to enter after him, but is trapped between a double portcullis. However, a maiden who had been to Arthur's court, and whom he had treated kindly, sees his plight and rescues him. Ywain sees the lady of the castle from his hiding-place; she is mourning for the death of her husband from the wound Ywain had given him, but the latter none the less falls in love with her. Lunet, the maiden who had helped him, eventually persuades her mistress to marry him, so that he can defend the fountain against Arthur's approaching army. This is done within a short time of her husband's death.

Arthur now arrives, and Ywain overthrows Kay before revealing his identity. He then entertains the King at his castle; but, urged by Gawain, he then leaves his lady, Alundyne, in search of further adventures, although she warns him that if he is absent for more than a year, she will cease to love him. Ywain forgets this, and when Lunet appears at Arthur's court to remind him, and to take back the magic ring that Alundyne had given him, he goes mad with grief, roaming the forests naked, and being fed by a hermit. A maiden finds him and brings him to her lady, who anoints him with a magic salve. He is cured, and defends the lady's castle for her, but refuses to wed her. He departs hastily, and rescues a lion from a fire-breathing serpent: it becomes his constant companion, so devoted to him that it attempts to kill itself when it thinks him dead. He is henceforth known as the 'Knight of the Lion'.

With the lion's assistance, he rescues the family of Gawain's sister, and saves Lunet from being burnt at the stake for treason. He begs her in return to try and appease Alundyne. Meanwhile, he is being sought as champion by the younger of two sisters who are quarrelling over the property left to them by their father.

GAWAIN 113

Gawain has been engaged to fight for the elder one. The younger
sister finds him, but they are both imprisoned. He escapes with
the lion's help, and kills the two giants who wrongfully hold the
castle, thereby winning the lord's daughter and all the lands
around. But he refuses both, and goes with the maiden to fulfil
his promise. The fight between him and Gawain lasts until
nightfall, and neither seems the stronger. They recognize each
other and make peace. The King divides the property equally
between the two sisters.

Ywain, lovesick for Alundyne, goes to the fountain and raises
the storm. Alundyne has no champion to oppose him. Lunet
says the 'Knight of the Lion' will fight for her on condition that
she will reconcile him with his wife. Alundyne readily agrees,
and when she discovers that this knight is in fact Ywain, she is
true to her promise, and all ends well.

The English work, though one of the longer English romances
—4,000 lines in length—is only a little over half the size of its
original. Chrétien's work is full of his usual introspective monologues, psychological digressions, and general discourses to his
audience, usually on love, which were not to the taste of the English. The translator accordingly condensed those parts of the
romance, while retaining the full plot: yet, unlike some later
writers, he did not entirely excise them. He replaced indirect
by direct speech and shortened unnecessary detail, but in comparison with the ordinary English poem of this type, the psychology of the characters is still very much in evidence. His
verse and style are for the most part of a reasonable standard, but
the vocabulary is limited and repetitive.

It is Ywain who is the real hero of the work and indeed he
dominates it throughout: the title *Ywain and Gawain* is misleading, and was probably altered from the French in order to
attract the English audience, with whom Gawain was much more
popular than on the other side of the Channel. But there is no
corresponding revision of the story to give more prominence to
the latter. Yvain himself is another of the historical Celtic heroes

I

of Arthurian romance.[17] The chieftain Owain ap Urien, son of the King of Rheged, an area in north England or south Scotland, fought against the Saxons with some success *c*. 580–600, and was celebrated by Taliesin and Llywarch Hen in Welsh poetry. It was via Brittany that the story reached Chrétien, as the name Yvain shows, since it corresponds to Breton Ivan rather than Welsh Owain.

Arthur is not quite the *roi fainéant*, the idle king, whose court is the centre of chivalry, and whose personal glory is mainly reflected, for this romance does allow him some part in the action —he leads the expedition to the fountain, and is only dissuaded with difficulty from jousting himself. His chief function is none the less as focal point around which the numerous characters assemble. It is interesting that here, in the most civilized of Arthurian works, and likewise in the most primitive ballads, that he plays a similar role, and only in pseudo-history does he come into his own.

The second poem of this group, *The Gest of Sir Gawain*,[18] a fifteenth-century poem from the south midlands, of which we have only the last 541 verses, is a translation from the first of the two continuations of Chrétien's unfinished *Conte del Graal*.

The beginning is lacking in the only manuscript, but we learn from the French original that Gawain has come to a pavilion in which he finds a fair lady. She has heard of him and worships him as the best of knights. They are making love as the English version opens. The lady's father arrives and finds them lying together, on which he forces Gawain to fight him. Gawain is victor, and the other knight departs. He meets his sons, who fight Gawain in turn. The first two are defeated, but the third, Brandelis, is a match for Gawain, and the outcome is undecided. They agree to meet again, but the English poet concludes by saying:

> 'And after that time they never met more;
> Full glad were those knights therefore.'

In the French poem, there is a sequel later; they fight again but the lady intervenes, and peace is made.

The continuation of the *Conte del Graal* has two versions of the incident, which are somewhat at variance. In the first, the lady has long admired Gawain without having seen him, and succumbs willingly to his advances. In the second, though at first consenting, she finally resists him, but in vain. For this outrage, first her brother, then her father, attack Gawain and are defeated; the first version has the order reversed. The English poet has combined the two, following the first in that the lady offers no resistance and receives him favourably, the second in that the father finds them together, and Gawain tries to make amends. The outcome of the jousts is also changed; none of the contestants is killed, and, most important, the entire sequel of Gawain and Brandelis's encounter is omitted.

But, although he has made a selection, the translator has added nothing new. The dialogue is all present in the French, and there is little else to the poem. It throws some light on the English taste in these matters, for we know that this was a popular story in Elizabethan times, both from a printed fragment which survives, and from two licences to print it granted about 1580 to two different printers within a comparatively short time.

A Scottish work from the same French source, *Golagrus and Gawain*,[19] represents a similar technique of adaptation, and is of about the same period, 1450–1500. Two incidents are chosen, but in the original they have no connection with each other. Together they form a poem 1,362 lines in length.

King Arthur is in Tuscany with a large and richly equipped army on his way to Jerusalem. He comes to a mountainous waste, and in crossing it, loses all his provisions. However, on reaching the other side, he sees a city, and proposes to send a messenger to ask the lord whether he may rest there. Kay volunteers, and, entering the castle, finds it empty save for a dwarf roasting some birds on a spit. Being hungry, Kay seizes them, but the lord appears and gives him such a blow that he is laid out on the floor.

When he recovers, he rides back to Arthur and tells him that nothing is to be gained from him. Gawain says that Kay is renowned for his rudeness and asks permission to try again, which he does with complete success, and the lord of the castle submits to Arthur as vassal of his own free will. After resting there for a few days, the King continues on his way.

They come to another castle, and Arthur, on inquiring as to its lord, is told by Sir Spinagros that he has never done homage to anyone. Arthur swears to make him his vassal on his return from Jerusalem. Some time later, in accordance with this vow, he comes back, and Gawain, Lancelot and Ywain are sent to the lord, Golagros; but persuasion fails, and Arthur besieges the castle. Two single combats are fought, and honours are even, followed by two combats between four knights of each side, again without result. Golagros then decides to fight himself, and Gawain opposes him. The duel is long, but Gawain eventually defeats Golagros, who asks to be killed, since none of his kin have ever before been defeated. Gawain is reluctant, and agrees to pretend that he has been defeated instead. Golagros promises that his honour will not be harmed as a result. They go into the castle, and Arthur, believing that Gawain has surrendered, is much grieved. But Golagros asks his vassals whether they would still accept him as lord after he had been defeated, and when they affirm their allegiance, acknowledges Gawain as victor. He does homage to Arthur, and holds a great feast for him. Arthur, before departing, releases him from his allegiance.

The poem is purely a glorification of Gawain. In the first half, Kay acts as a foil to him in the incident known as 'Kay and the Spit', and Gawain's courtesy is emphasized. The second half culminates in the duel between Golagros and Gawain, in which Gawain's courage and generosity are brought out. While retaining the general form of the French, the writer has, in contrast to the two translators whose works have just been discussed, treated his subjects with some freedom, certainly as far as detail is concerned.

Archaic forms abound in the rather limited vocabulary, and the Scottish dialect is much in evidence. As so often with alliterative verse, the battle scenes are the strongest point of the work: description of other kinds is also good. There is a vigour and clarity often lacking in translations. Here is part of his description of Gawain's battle with Golagros:

> With ane bitand brand, burly and braid,
> Whilk oft in battale had been his bute, and his belde,
> He leit gird to the grome, with greif that he had,
> And claif throw the cantell of the clene schelde;
> Throw birny, and breist-plait, and bordour, it baid;
> The fulie of the fine gold fell in the feild.
> The rede blude with the rout folowit the blaid,
> For all the wedis, I wise, that the wy weild,
> Throw claspis of clene gold, and clowis sa clair,
> Thair with schir Gologras the sire,
> In mekill anger and ire
> Alse ferse as the fire,
> Leit fle to his feir.*

Our last poem is usually included in the group with Arthur as central figure. But the title, *The Awntyrrs of Arthur,*† is misleading, for Gawain is very much its hero. It is in the same metre as *Golagros and Gawain*, but is two hundred years earlier, and from the north of England. It has been ascribed to Huchown of the Awle Ryale, on the strength of Wyntoun's assertion in Book 5 of his *Chronykil of Scotland* that among this writer's works was an *Awntyre of Gawane*. Although this could well apply to the present poem, the identification is doubtful.

* With a keen sword, sturdy and sharp, which had often been his companion and stay in battle, he attacked the man, furious with pain, and cut through the cantell of his bright shield; through his mail and breast-plate and border it went; the ornament of gold fell to the ground. Red blood gushed out along the blade, in spite of all the armour he was wearing, it went through gold clasps and bright fastenings. At this Sir Golagros in great wrath and anger, fierce as fire, let fly at his foe.

† 'The Adventures of Arthur'.

Arthur is out hunting near the Tarn Wadeling, and leaves Guinevere with Gawain. At midday there is a sudden darkness and a ghost appears to them. Gawain tries to reassure the Queen, and proceeds to question the ghost, who reveals herself as Guinevere's mother. She says that she is now in torment because of a vow she broke. Guinevere asks if anything can be done for her and is told that a million masses said for her soul will release her. Guinevere promises to have this done. The ghost then foretells in some detail Mordred's treachery and Arthur's end, and vanishes. The darkness clears: the king rejoins them, and they return together to Carlisle. As they are banqueting there, a knight accompanied by his lady appears, and asks for an audience of the King. Arthur inquires as to his mission, and the knight explains that he is Sir Galeron, lord of some lands in Galloway that Arthur has given to Gawain. He challenges Gawain to a joust to decide who shall have the lands. The joust is long and indecisive; both knights are badly wounded. Guinevere intervenes and it is stopped. Both knights acknowledge the other as victor, but Gawain finally prevails upon Galeron to accept the lands. Galeron is made knight of the Round Table, and the million masses for Guinevere's mother are duly said.

This poem is either the original of, or part of, the group which connect Arthur with the countryside around Carlisle. 'Tarn Wathelyne' or 'Wadeling' which occurs also in *The Wedding of Sir Gawain* and *The Avowing of Arthur* is a small lake in Inglewood Forest, near Hesketh, in Cumberland. This forest also appears in other poems, and *Sir Gawain and the Carl of Carlisle* provides yet another link.

How this association arose in the first place is a mystery. The English stanzaic *Le Mort Arthur* of the same period places the scene of the Lancelot and Guinevere episodes at Carlisle, but whether this was in the French original is uncertain, since we possess only a related version, and not the version from which it was directly taken. It is possible that a French corruption of Caerleon or Carduel was rendered as Carlisle.

The Awntyrrs of Arthur, is, as far as we can tell, original.
Parallels to it, however, are found in the incident in *The Trentals
of Pope Gregory* in which the Pope's mother appears and requests
a 'trental' of masses, like Guinevere's mother in the present case.
The combat between Gawain and Galeron was probably inspired by a *chanson de geste*. Gawain's association with Galloway,
an important feature of this latter incident, is of considerable
antiquity. William of Malmesbury, in recording the discovery of
his supposed grave in Pembrokeshire, remarks on it, and it seems
to have come from Welsh legend.

The characters of the various knights are still in an intermediate stage. Gawain retains his position as first knight of
Arthur's court, yet there is French influence in the portrait of
Guinevere. As far as style and powers of description are concerned, it is one of the better English poems: there is some
dramatic power in the account of the ghost's appearance, and it
is evident that this appealed to the writer's imagination rather
more than the duel later in the poem.

We may pause here to review the progress of Gawain's character. From an unimportant role in the *Historia Regum Britanniae*,
he rises to the position of first knight of Arthur's court in the
early French romances, skilled in knightly arts but by no means
faultless. The English writers raised him a stage further and portrayed him as the perfect knight; his morals are not always
impeccable, but on one occasion at least this is out of courtesy
to his host. And in *Sir Gawain and the Green Knight* both
English romance and its greatest individual hero reach their
climax.

But if we look forward to Malory and Tennyson, the picture
changes drastically. The French, in making Lancelot their chief
Arthurian hero, later debased Gawain's character, and he is made
to bear a large part of the blame for the disintegration of the
Round Table. Drawing on their work, Malory calls him,
Mordred, Agravaine and Gaheris 'murtherars of good knightes',
but does give one moment of greatness in his last letter to

Lancelot. Tennyson also regards him as one of the worse elements in Arthur's court. Such was the tragic fate of the earliest of the great Arthurian figures; but before this came about, he enjoyed the praise of the best of the medieval English poets.

With this we complete our survey of the English romances. A steady mediocrity, with occasional lapses into crudity, and only one major masterpiece, is the sum of their literary achievement. Yet they are not without interest as a mirror of taste, and some of the stories are considerably stronger in plot than those Malory has to tell, even though the execution is far less distinguished. They never achieved the same enormous popularity as in France, even in the rare cases where they were on a similar literary level to that of their continental counterparts, and are therefore far less numerous. We have discussed all the reasonably complete works that are extant in the foregoing pages, and it should be evident why they did not endure long after the English Renaissance. In spirit they belong to the Middle Ages, and possess more of its faults than its virtues. But they are by no means lifeless, and offer us a good opportunity of observing one aspect of the workings of the medieval mind.

The year 1500 is the upper limit of composition of the English romances. This does not imply a complete cessation of interest in them, and they were certainly read in Elizabethan days, as we know from printers' licences. Further debasement of the originals continued, and there are several ballads which may be briefly mentioned. All except two are printed in *Percy's Reliques*.

The Legend of King Arthur[20] is an abridgement in 110 verses of the chronicle story of Arthur as found in that of de Leeuw, printed in Amsterdam in 1493. Lancelot appears, but otherwise there is little variation from Geoffrey of Monmouth. The Percy folio version of *Sir Gawain and the Carl of Carlisle* has already been mentioned, and there is also a very defective ballad of *The Wedding of Sir Gawain, The Marriage of Sir Gawain*.[21]

Sir Lancelot du Lake[22] is apparently the fragment of a longer ballad. It is probably based on Malory, and tells of Lancelot's fight with Tarquin. Similarly, *King Arthur's Death*[23] is from Malory, or one of his sources, *Le Mort Arthur*. The latter seems to present a closer version. The roles of Lucan and Bedivere are reversed; the ending has certain affinities with Layamon, but these are probably fortuitous.

Two ballads whose immediate sources have been lost complete the collection. *King Arthur and King Cornwall*,[24] so defective as to be of little value as a story, is of interest in that Sir Bredbeddle, the Green Knight in the later version of *Sir Gawain and the Green Knight*, appears in it. His name may have been transferred in error by the scribe to the *Greene Knight* which is in the same manuscript. Sir Marramile, Tristram's companion, is a corruption of 'Marhalt miles', the Irish champion defeated by Tristram.

Lastly, we have *The Boy and the Mantle*[25] whose central figure, Carados or Cradock, is well known in French and Welsh romance. The test of the horn is found in Malory,[26] where it has been taken from the *Prose Tristan*. Here Morgan le Fay sends it to Arthur, but it is intercepted and sent to Mark. Caxton refers to Cradock's mantle as being at Dover in his preface to Malory, which shows that a romance version of the story was probably known to him.

Thus ended the age of Arthurian romance proper in England. From the heights of *Sir Gawain and the Green Knight* it had declined considerably to the purely popular and the uninspired translation. Yet before it finally passed there was to appear one of the most masterly versions of the legends in any language, one of the great prose works of England. Without this group of tales, the Arthurian tradition in later days would have taken a very different course, if indeed it had survived at all. It is to this last flowering of romance that we now turn.

SEVEN

THE FLOWER OF CHIVALRY

SIR THOMAS MALORY'S renderings of the French prose romances are the first and only reproduction of a coherent cycle in English, retaining the major features of the stories, yet rejecting those unsuitable or over-lengthy for the English taste. Indeed, only one other anonymous writer had attempted an English prose translation of any part of these works. But, just as it had been in the prose versions that the French romances had attained their greatest popularity, so it was in Malory's works—albeit in edited form—that the romances reached their highest esteem in England.

Before discussing his works, a portrait of Malory himself is essential. And in this lies one of the strangest paradoxes in English literature. Sir Thomas Malory, writer of one of the great expositions of the ideals of chivalry, was a common criminal, and his 'noble tales' were written during a prison sentence.* Yet this imputes in no wise on the tone of his book, for it seems to have been something approaching an act of contrition on his part.

It is of course conceivable that another and contemporary Sir Thomas Malory was the writer, but there is no evidence to show that it was any other than the only knight of this name of whom we have record. He was born at Newbold Revell in Warwickshire *c.* 1410. At the age of about twenty-three he inherited the

* See the colophons of Books IV and XXI (O.S.A. edition).

family estates, and in the following year served at Calais under the Earl of Warwick, with one lancer and two archers. He married in about 1440, and had one son, who died within his father's lifetime. It is just conceivable that this, or some similar tragedy sparked off what a biographer[1] has called his 'orgy of lawlessness'. Between June 1450 and July 1451 he committed a dozen crimes including attempted murder, theft, rape, and extortion. He was arrested and imprisoned at Coleshill in July 1451, but escaped within a day or two by swimming the moat; his recapture took place, after further robberies, in the following month. He spent the next three years in prison, except for a brief interval in 1452. However, on his release on bail in May 1454, he continued his career of crime in Essex. In October of the same year he was imprisoned in Colchester Castle, and was unable to appear at the expiry of his bail. He was handed over to the Marshal in November, and we know nothing more until February 1456, when he produced a writ of pardon issued by the Duke of York during his period of office as Lord Protector in November 1455 in answer to the charges against him. The following month he borrowed a sum of money, and sat for his shire in Parliament. He apparently failed to repay the debt, for he was imprisoned in Ludgate until October 1457, when he was once more released on bail. At the end of two months he returned to prison. The date of his release is not certain, but in 1459 he was apparently at large in Warwickshire. In Lent 1460 he was recaptured and imprisoned in Newgate.

This was to be his last criminal imprisonment, and in 1462 he accompanied the Earl of Warwick on Edward IV's expedition to Northumberland, and was at Bamborough and Alnwick* with him during the sieges. There is reason to believe that he joined the Lancastrians when Warwick broke with Edward IV, and was active in the campaign against the latter, for he is excluded specifically from two general pardons to the Lancastrians granted in 1467. His final imprisonment in 1469-70 seems to have been

---

* Cf. the references in Book XXI, p. 881 (O.S.A. edition).

for political reasons; it is this period that produced all the great stories which have ensured his fame. Whether he was released before his death on March 14th, 1471, we cannot tell, but he is buried not far from the prison, in Greyfriars Church.

In its original version, the work known as the *Morte Darthur* was in fact eight separate books. For some three and a half centuries, Caxton's edition, which welds them into one, albeit not very coherent, single composition, was regarded as being a more or less faithful reproduction of the original. In 1934, however, there came to light in the Winchester College Fellows' Library a unique MS. version of the eight tales, which for the first time revealed the true nature of Malory's composition.

We know from the fact that there is no continuous chronology throughout the work that these tales were conceived independently; for, although there are no contradictions within each of the units, we find the birth of Sir Tristram related three hundred pages after his first appearance. Caxton, in his eagerness to present these stories as a single composition, imposed a false unity by omitting the colophon to each, and by abbreviation. This unity, so often praised by earlier critics,* is of a very different kind from that conceived until now, and bears a closer resemblance to the Vulgate Cycle from which Malory took his material.

The immediate question which springs to mind is: 'Did Malory intend the works to be placed in the order in which they appear in Caxton, and, if so, did he write them in that order?' The first part can almost certainly be answered in the affirmative. The Winchester MS. shows that Caxton's order was probably correct, as it is identical. However, we can tell from internal evidence[2] that the first two were composed in reverse order, *The Tale of King Arthur and the Emperor Lucius* antedating *The Tale of King Arthur*. We have no method of determining the order in which *The Tale of Gareth* and *The Tale of Lancelot* were

* E.g. 'Of this vast assemblage of stories only Malory makes one story and one book.' (*The English Novel*, London, 1913, p. 25.)

composed, and these might easily be reversed, though in the lack of other evidence we may assume that the order in sequence is that of composition.

The Tale of King Arthur and the Emperor Lucius, is Malory's first literary effort which we possess. It is an almost straight-forward modernization in prose of the English alliterative chronicle known as the Thornton *Morte Arthure*, examined in the previous chapter. This epic-heroic work had great influence on his later style. There is virtually none of the recomposition and rearrangement found in his later works, as the narrative of the poem is direct and uncomplicated and some of the lines are directly quoted.* It is here that Caxton has made the most considerable abbreviation, possibly because he felt that the source might be recognized, and his version bears very little resemblance to what Malory actually wrote.

In view of the close copying of the original, it is strange to find here another example of the contemporary reference process found in Geoffrey of Monmouth's work and in the Thornton *Morte Arthure* itself. Malory's efforts in this direction are not so radical as those of his predecessors, of whose alterations in all probability he knew nothing. Arthur is modelled in some respects on Henry V, as is suggested by his route through France,[3] which is reminiscent of the campaign preceding Agincourt. Instead of Mordred, two chieftains are left as regents, in much the same way as Henry left Beaufort and Bedford. In addition, Arthur is actually crowned by the Pope, a parallel to Henry VI's French coronation. The only other alteration, which will be discussed at greater length at a later stage, is the new prominence of Lancelot as a warrior-hero, replacing Gawain in the original. This may have been part of a later revision, when the character of Mordred and the final scenes, which must have been in his earliest version of it, were also removed.

Malory then turned to the French romances, with which he

---

* See Vinaver's editions where such lines are marked with two opposed half-diagonal lines: ` \/ `.

had probably become acquainted during his campaigning in France. He seems to have obtained a composite volume containing most of the Vulgate Cycle. The first romance in it was in fact from the *Roman du Graal*, and is known as the Huth-Merlin; it differs substantially from the Vulgate *Estoire de Merlin*, and includes the *Suite du Merlin*, but is nevertheless perfectly compatible with the other branches of the Vulgate Cycle.

On reading the French, he must have discovered very rapidly that a very different story-telling technique was involved as compared to the familiar and direct style of the English writer. A number of themes were interwoven in an almost inextricable way, giving a tapestry-like effect to the whole. Quite frequently, the themes or their sequels extended between separate romances, thus giving the Vulgate Cycle—and Malory's eight tales—their unity. Malory succeeded in isolating many of the incidents, yet he was unable to sever some of the links; these latter he strengthened to some extent, especially if they provided a point of contact between his tales. This process is well illustrated by the *Tale of Balin and Balan*. To the original story has been attached the Dolorous Blow incident, which occurs quite separately in the French. This unifies the tale, and strengthens its theme of Balin as a fated knight. It is chiefly this method of handling the material which distinguishes the *Tale of King Arthur* from a mere translation. He has also suppressed the Morgan le Faye and Merlin themes, and brought Arthur into greater prominence.

Lancelot, as we have seen, first appears in the *Tale of King Arthur and the Emperor Lucius*, and this puts his story in a different light. He now first achieves fame by his military exploits in the Roman Wars,* and goes on to become first knight of the Round Table in deeds of chivalry afterwards, whereas the French cycle reversed this process. His position as Guinevere's lover, the role in which his character first became of importance,‡ is suppressed slightly by Malory, who felt it to be out of keeping.

* In the French, these did not occur until the last book, *La Mort Artu.*
† Cf. Chrétien de Troyes's *Chevalier de la Charrette.*

The Tale of Sir Lancelot du Lake falls into three sections.[4] The first of these is the third part of the French *Livres del Lancelot.* Malory has reduced it by approximately half, while retaining the outline of the original. He then moves to the next reference to the Lancelot-Lionel theme, separated by many pages in the original, containing cyclic material on other themes. He omits this latter *en bloc.* The third section has no known source, but it is probable that Malory followed with the same degree of closeness a version of the romance now lost. The Chapel Perilous episode is closely paralleled by that in the French romance *Perlesvaus,** save for the damsel's motive, but this is unlikely to be the direct original. The sections chosen from this unknown work deal entirely with adventures pure and simple, without any underlying theme. The conclusion, as so often, is Malory's own, and probably cuts short his source by a considerable amount.[5]

For *The Tale of Sir Gareth* we are completely without a source. The *Libeaus Desconus* story bears some resemblance, and the *La Cote Male Taille* incident in the French *Prose Tristan* may have contributed to it. This latter, a vast compilation of Arthurian incidents tenuously connected by the figures of the Tristram and Iseult story, gave Gawain his bad name, and it is not until we reach the last section of Malory's work that he regains his earlier character. The original of 'Gareth' seems to have been either a self-contained incident in this work, or alternatively an interpolation.[6]

This book is the shortest unit of Malory's works; the next, *The Book of Sir Tristram de Lyones* represents between one-third and one-half of his entire output. It is directly based on the *Prose Tristan* already mentioned, and from various portions of four different MSS. the entire version used by Malory can be reconstructed.

Malory now begins to treat his material with increasing freedom and confidence. He firmly omits the entire third book,

* Translated by S. Evans as the *High History of the Holy Grail.* Temple Classics, 1912.

which dealt with some of the Grail adventures, and admits this in his colophon.[7] The introduction concerned with Tristram's ancestors has also been ignored, and the whole is divided into sections, marked by an Incipit and Explicit in the Winchester MS.

He has not altered the literary style of the French so much as its character. The Tristram story is not a tragedy: we only learn of the death of the lovers—in a very different version from the earliest and best known one—by a chance remark in the last part of *Lancelot and Guinevere*. The tragic undertones throughout have been removed, partly by entirely blackening Mark's character, and hence giving Tristram every right to love Iseult. Tristram becomes above all a knight; his love for Iseult is an adjunct of his chivalry and not the prime motive of his life. The return of the lovers to Joyous Gard is Malory's own invention to replace the French ending. This replacement of *amour courtois* by his own type of chivalry is typical of Malory; yet he fails to remove Sir Dinadan entirely, who scoffs at just that attitude to life engendered by such a code, and has to be content with reducing his appearances to a minimum.

Some of Malory's sections are interpolations into the *Prose Tristan* from other sources, which he has adopted without hesitation. Such are the stories of Alexander the Orphan and the Tournament at Surluse, both from the fourteenth-century *Prophéties de Merlin*, and the story of Lancelot and Elaine, from the *Livres del Lancelot*. The final section comes almost directly from the French, but there it is not in fact the end of the story, as has been remarked above.

The original of the *Tale of the Sankgreall*, the French Vulgate *Queste del Saint Graal*, follows the *Livres del Lancelot* in the cycle, and forms its fourth branch. We have no manuscript which exactly corresponds to the passages selected from it by Malory, but there are no great differences in actual material. His skill here has been directed at omissions calculated to alter entirely the character of the Quest. The French work was virtually an exposition of the doctrine of Grace and Salvation, and to emphasize and interpret the moral of each adventure, hermits appear on every other page, who, while attending to the injuries of the defeated knight, give one or more sermons on the sins which were responsible for his downfall. Malory has ruthlessly excised most of these, and abbreviated the moralizings of the remainder. In doing so, he manages to make the Grail adventures much more to the credit of Lancelot and the chivalry which he represents, thus uniting the secular and celestial types of the latter. The religious atmosphere of purification and repentance is removed; and Lancelot's relative success is emphasized rather than his eventual failure in the vital part of the Quest. Such treatment may be bad theology, but it helps to give the story an atmosphere more compatible with the rest of the cycle.

For the last two of his eight tales, Malory combined English and French romances, but depended less and less on his sources. The two works he used were the *Le Mort Arthur* and the conclusion of the Vulgate Cycle *La Mort Artu.** In the *Book of Sir Launcelot and Queen Guinevere*, the first two parts are taken almost directly from these romances, although they are carefully selected. But from here onwards he departs from any known version of either French or English. In *The Great Tournament*, for example, the last part, describing the actual tournament, is Malory's own work, and *The Knight of the Cart* is very much rewritten, for in the original, Chrétien de Troyes's *Le Chevalier de la Charrette*, great shame was attached to Lancelot's journey in the cart, this being the usual conveyance to the scaffold; but here it is merely another adventure. Finally, *The Healing of Sir Urry* is entirely his own invention. Here he brings in almost all the knights whose names he had come across in his wide reading, a triumphant fanfare of names that is a roll-call of Arthur's company.

* Professor Vinaver, in his edition of the Winchester MS. (O.U.P. 1947) to which any writer on Malory today must be greatly indebted, rejects Malory's use of *Le Mort Arthur*; but this has been shown to be incorrect.[8]

K

Until now, in spite of the *Tale of the Sankgreall*, Malory had had relatively little trouble in making Lancelot his hero. But when he came to the tragic conclusion of the cycle, he found that Lancelot was the main agent of Arthur's downfall, according to the French writers. Malory could not blame him for this without destroying his position as the ideal of chivalry; nor did the blunt statement at the end of the previous tale solve the problem: 'and now I go unto the morte Arthur, and that caused sir Aggravayne '. He had to make a major alteration to the old tale, and he effected this by standing back from all moral judgments, thus shifting the emphasis on to character and situation rather than cause and effect. The feeling throughout the last book is that of a series of accidents, combined with regret and longing for what might have been. The tragic aspect is well brought out by heightening the intimacy of the relationship between Lancelot, Guinevere, Arthur and Gawain. Loyalty plays an important part; Lancelot's loyalty to Guinevere, and Gawain's loyalty to kith and kin are both major forces in the disaster.

The conclusion is the most brilliant part of the work. The writer of *La Mort Artu* became over-florid and the English writer insipid, when confronted with this problem; but it is here that Malory's prose reaches its majestic climax of greatness and grief. His revision of the incidents of the last stages of the disaster is done with much finesse and feeling, especially where Lancelot's death is concerned. The French version makes him die, rather uncharacteristically, of religious devotion, but Malory makes it his enduring love for Guinevere. A certain premonition of disaster before the great battle between Arthur and Mordred, heightens the tension; the aftermath shows the totality and human intensity of the tragedy.

In the latter half, Malory's great technical advance is also most evident. The medieval writers were usually more concerned with meanings than events, a trait seen at its worst in the French *Queste del Saint Graal*. Tales were either fantasies irrelevant to real life or moral illustrations, and the Arthurian legend had been used as both. Malory has achieved a reality that requires no moral standpoint as its excuse or purpose, and has turned to the interplay of character and situation instead. Yet this absence of moral does not mean that he has no hero, but that he has a hero who is all too fallible. And this also works in reverse; for he does not seem to have set out with the conscious intention of writing a story without a moral standpoint. He arrived at this by a process of evolution. It would be no great exaggeration to say that, having chosen Lancelot as his ideal, he altered everything to harmonize with this, and to show him in a better light where necessary. Hence it is chivalry rather than *amour courtois* in which his practical nature is interested, and he does his best to divorce the two. This led him into major difficulties, for in the French romances the two are quite inseparable. His answer to the problem lies in Lancelot's speech to the damsel whom he rescues from Sir Perrys. The latter reproves him for having neither wife nor mistress. He replies: '. . . for to be a wedded man, I thynke hit nat, for than I muste couche with hir and leve armys and turnamentis, batellys and adventures. And as for to sey to take my pleasaunce with peramours, that woll I refuse: in prencipall for drede of God, for knyghtes that bene adventures sholde nat be advoutrers nothir lecherous, for than hey be nat happy nother fortunate unto the werrys; for other they shall be overcom with a sympler knyght than they be hemself, other ellys they shall sle by unhappe and hir cursednesse bettir men than they be hemself. And so who that usyth peramours shall be unhappy, and all thynge unhappy that is about them.' Love is in fact totally incompatible with adventures, instead of being their ultimate object. The High Order of Knighthood is the great theme of Malory, and its code his ideal, as far as a code which is merely the upholding of certain practical laws towards others, whatever the danger, can be an ideal.

From this, achievements tend to be measured in terms of personal valour, and valour is rated on a 'Lancelot scale'. Lancelot is the best, and the rest are judged by how nearly they approach him. Yet Lancelot is overthrown by his son, Galahad, in the *Tale of the Sankgreall*. In view of the earlier part of the book, this seems scarcely credible, and Lancelot himself is stunned by it; but Malory does not transfer the central place to Galahad. His code of knighthood has become involved with forces above it and beyond it; and he merely accepts the moral he finds in the French and carries on as before, putting the earthly worship attached to the Grail quest before its religious object and spiritual benefit. His lack of enthusiasm for Galahad and Percival is noteworthy, and springs from the same cause as his rejection of *amour courtois*: he prefers the practical to the ethereal and spiritual.

Since he accepts the French writer's judgment when he finds anything that lies outside the scope of the chivalric code he acquires a triple scale of values, and Lancelot's position varies on each. He is best on the chivalric side; he is good from the point of view of *amour courtois*, and bad when it comes to the theological side.

So there arises a hero who is fallible, an important step towards the modern novel. But how has Malory presented the rest of the scene, the other characters and situations? The situations also mark a great advance, for throughout the eight tales, each theme is dealt with singly as one incident, with very few exceptions. His singleness of purpose in following out these episodes is all the more remarkable when one turns to the French and finds one story in Malory split into three parts hundreds of pages apart. This unravelling of the threads of the Vulgate Cycle and gathering of them into one simple pattern is Malory's hardest-won victory.

Lastly, his remodellings have brought out the traits of the characters in sharper relief. Arthur, we feel, would without doubt have been his hero, had the French stories contained enough material to give him a suitable glory in knightly exploits. As it is, he is hero of the first two stories, and Malory pays him the highest compliment he can: 'of him all knights may learn to be a knight'. Guinevere, like all Malory's female characters, lacks life and conviction; her only function in the French romances was to be Lancelot's lover, and this Malory denies her to a great extent. Neither is she Arthur's queen in more than title, for Arthur's great interest is his company of knights. In the final stages of the tragedy he says: 'And much more I am sorrier for the loss of my good knights than for the loss of my queen; for queens I might have enow, but such a fellowship of good knights shall never be together in any company.'

Gawain has been replaced by Lancelot to a great extent, yet in the loss of position he has gained in character: impetuous, quick to repent, courageous, yet unfortunate in his deeds, he is in some ways more human and sympathetic than Lancelot, though Malory tends to emphasize his worst side. His final letter to Lancelot is one of the most moving moments of the eight tales. The other knights fall into one of the three groups: either they are the Lancelot type, without quite the perfection of knightly skill, or the Gawain type, meaning well but unfortunate in their actions. Finally, there is the Galahad type, whom Malory does not regard favourably, and whom he divests of any humanly attractive traits.

Merlin and Morgan le Faye play a less important part in Malory than in the French romances, for two reasons. Firstly, the demand for the grotesque and incredible was not a trait of Malory's class or times, but rather of the medieval mind. Secondly, the magic element was incongruous in the French romances, and in his simplification of the latter he naturally rejected it. Once again, his attitude is more modern than his material, and he has removed another of the old motive forces in the tragedy without replacing it.

Thus out of the diffuseness of the Vulgate Cycle, with its recurrent themes and unwieldy branches, Malory forged a coherent whole, cutting away the multiplication of incidents that have no real value as far as the main plot is concerned, and drastically abbreviating the wordy disquisitions on love, religion and chivalry which had encumbered the romances. The prose of the French was, like the frame of their work, an unwieldy tapestry. Out of this Malory drew short phrases with a clear cadence. His prose is crisp, lucid and rhythmic, varying in tone with the events it describes: quick and fierce for a combat:

'So whan Sir Launcelot saw his party go so to the warre, he thrange oute to the thyckyst with a bygge swerde in his honde. And there he smote downe on the ryght honde and on the lyffte honde, and pulled down knyghtes and russhed of helmys that all men had wondir that ever knyght myght do suche dedis of armis.'

Or it can become elegiac and solemn in grief:

'And now I dare say, thou sir Launcelot, there thou lyest, that thou were never matched of erthely knyghtes hande. And thou were the curtest knyght that ever bare shelde! And thou were the truest frende to thy lovar that ever bestrade hors, and thou were the trewest lover of a synful man that ever loved woman, and thou were the kyndest man that ever strake with swerde. And thou were the godelyest perone that ever cam emonge prees of knyghtes, and thou was the mekest man and the jentyllest that ever ete in halle emonge ladyes, and thou were the sternest knyght to thy mortal foo that ever put spere in the reeste.

'Than there was wepyng and dolour out of mesure.'

With these two new qualities of unity and clarity in the telling of the stories of which it is made up, the noble tragedy of Arthur stands out once again from the mass of adventures and marvels in which it had become entangled. Its protagonists become real people; its events are the more dramatic stripped of their moral or fatalistic overtones; and the climax has a befitting majesty and grandeur that it had never attained before. The old traditions gain new vigour; for in the Vulgate Cycle lay hidden a great epic drama, ranging through every human passion, joy and grief. But it needed Malory's skilful hand to reveal the full force of its 'noble chyvalrye, curtosye, humanyté, frendlynesse, hardynesse, love, frendshyp, cowardyse, murder, hate, vertue and synne'. By doing so, he ensured that the Arthurian tradition of England would not become a literary curiosity like the romances of Charlemagne and Alexander, but would re-emerge to inspire new masterpieces and to enrich yet further our literature; and this achievement was his alone.

EIGHT

REACTION AND REVIVAL

THREE centuries were to elapse before the Arthurian legend was once again to be studied and read with interest. The 'new learning' of the Renaissance brought with it reaction—a reaction to Geoffrey of Monmouth. For several decades, in fact for the best part of the sixteenth century, the *Historia Regum Britanniae* was to be accepted with very little objection, and belief in its accuracy persisted long after most serious writers had rejected it as a basis for history. Many works were drawn directly from it in the literary field.

However, this process was not completely immediate: two further works in the romance style were to show the way to further developments of the legend which were almost unconnected with Arthur. *The Litel Tretys of the Birth and Prophecies of Merlin* had many successors. The prophecies, though far more incredible than the average romance, remained a controversial centre of interest, if not belief, until the middle of the seventeenth century, and fulfilments of them were always being pointed out. The accession of James I was the occasion for much work on these lines, and two editions of the prophecies appeared during his reign. Camden in his *Remains Concerning Britain* quotes an anagram based on the popular identification of James with Arthur:

'Charles James Stuart
Claims Arthur's seat.'

136

Each of the Stuarts except the second James was to be thus iden-
tified. Prince Henry, James I's eldest son, was addressed as
'heir to Arthur's crown and chair', in Ben Jonson's *Masque of
Oberon*, where other Arthurian references are also to be found.
Charles I was represented by Arthur in a continuation of the
Faery Queen, which appeared in 1635. However, the prophecies
themselves were gradually discredited, partly by satires such as
Rowley's *The Birth of Merlin*.

Equally important in its consequences was Lord Berners's
translation of a popular fifteenth-century French romance,
Arthur of Little Britain, published *c.* 1530. The translation itself
does not approach his version of *Huon of Bordeaux*, but it is the
plot that holds the main interest for us. It is a fairy tale pure and
simple: Arthur becomes a lover who first sees his beloved in a
dream and seeks her human counterpart, a theme frequently
used since in various forms.* As might be expected in such a tale,
the atmosphere is even more unreal than in the most extravagant
of the earlier French Arthurian romances, and there is no characterization to speak of. The style is for the modern reader the
work's most entertaining feature, often literally picturesque and
always lively.

This same conception of Arthur, albeit in a further modified
form, recurs in Spenser's *Faery Queen*. The double alteration of
his character, once by the author of *Artus de Petit Bretagne* and
again by Spenser, gives a result with only the slimmest connections with the main stream of the legend. Spenser's Prince
Arthur is scarcely the same Arthur: and it has been suggested
that Henry VII's eldest son, of the same name, is the real reason
for Spenser's choice of hero. Malory's work has been only
slightly used, although some of the events of Book VI appear:
but there is very little contact between the two. To what degree
Spenser drew on *Arthur of Little Britain* is again hard to
determine with accuracy, but there can be no doubt that
the majority of the plot and characterization of *The Faery*

* Cf. the German writer, Novalis.

Queen being allegorical, must have come from the author's own hand.

If Spenser's Arthur is not the Arthur of romance, and leaving aside the idea of Henry VII's son as source, from what quarter might Spenser have got the idea of using him as hero? It seems that a combination of his still high reputation as a literary figure and—though we cannot be sure of this—Camden's remarks in 1585 that Arthur would be a suitable epic subject, may have suggested it to him. Camden was thinking of the historical Arthur, and Spenser may well have read the *Historia Regum Britanniae*. Even if his direct original was a mixture of Lord Berners's Arthur, with the Arthur imagined by patriotic antiquarians, he produced from it an idealized hero rather than a specific character.

The historical Arthur is also the subject of the only Arthurian play prior to 1890. 'The Misfortunes of Arthur'[1] was written in 1587 by Thomas Hughes for an entertainment at Gray's Inn before Queen Elizabeth I. It presents a straightforward outline of Arthur's life in the form of a tragedy in the style of Seneca, the basic plot being drawn from Geoffrey of Monmouth, with an occasional echo of Malory. Seneca is imitated to the extent of direct quotations, and the plot is shaped to match his. Arthur himself is the only character to rise above his Senecan prototype, but the play is often better reading than its modern successors.

If the sixteenth century has little Arthurian literature to show, there is scarcely more to be gleaned from the seventeenth than the prophecies and histories already mentioned and unfulfilled projects by major writers. Thomas Munday's translations of semi-Arthurian romances were very popular at the end of the sixteenth century, but there is little of interest in the first quarter of the seventeenth. Richard Johnson's *Romance of Tom a Lincolne, The Red Rose Knight* of *c.* 1610, presents as the hero of the title an illegitimate son of Arthur. The story is completely invented, and of little merit. Arthur and Lancelot are the only figures of importance beside the hero.

We now come to Milton's project for an Arthurian epic, to which considerable importance is sometimes attached. In fact, there are only two definite references to his intention of writing this work, in *To Manso* and *Epitaphium Damonis*, but his interest seems to have been keen for some time. But it was certainly never more than a project, and by the time he came to writing *Paradise Lost* and *Paradise Regained* he had grown sceptical, for there are but two brief remarks on Arthur here. In his *British History* he questions the very existence of Arthur, and pours scorn on the legends. It seems likely that on closer examination he found that the subject was not really to his liking, since there was no really firm basis of accepted story.

The Famous History of That Most Reverend Christian Worthy, Arthur of the Britons, and his famous Knights of the Round Table, by one Martin Parker, published in 1660, is about as fantastic as its title. It is a wildly improbable pseudo-historical romance, in which Arthur's exploits are multiplied and raised to an incredible level. He goes on a crusade to Palestine, and defeats the Saracens twelve times, killing over 40,000 at each of these encounters. It is probably only because the book is incomplete that he does not conquer Rome as well as the Holy Land.

The title of the previous book is explained by the account of Arthur in the *History of the Nine Christian Worthies* of 1687. The Nine Worthies, three classical, three pagan, and three Christian, were a popular subject in medieval art, Arthur being the first of the three Christian worthies. The other two were Charlemagne and Godfrey of Boulogne, King of Jerusalem. The usual pseudo-history is retold once more.

Another project not fulfilled in its original form was that mentioned by John Dryden in the preface to his translation of Juvenal. He states his intention of giving up his dramatic work in order to write an Arthurian epic. Financial conditions forced him to continue to write the more profitable plays, but his ideas took shape as a dramatic opera in collaboration with Purcell, 'King Arthur'. The first version had a political bias in support of Charles II, but since production was delayed until 1691, considerable alterations had to be made. In this process most of the real substance of the work was cut out, and its final form is a very free version of Arthur's struggle against the Saxons, treated in the same fairy-tale manner as his adaptation of *The Tempest* four years later. Enchantments play a large part in the rather strained plot, which was entirely invented by Dryden, and is in fact much too complicated for stage purposes.

The only real fulfilment of these plans for an Arthurian epic poem came from the pen of a minor writer, Sir Richard Blackmore. He was Physician in Ordinary to William III and took up the writing of epics as 'an innocent amusement to entertain me in such leisure hours as were usually past away before in Conversation and unprofitable telling and hearing of News'. He studied the efforts of previous epic writers and the rules that they followed, and set out to rival Homer and Virgil with his 'innocent amusement'.

His first effort, *Prince Arthur*, published in 1695, owes much to these studies. Milton and Virgil seem to be largely responsible. It presents an entirely new version of Arthur's conquest of Britain. Arthur has taken refuge on the Continent after Uther's overthrow by the Saxons, and at the opening of the poem is returning to England with a considerable host to regain his rightful inheritance. He is twice shipwrecked by diabolical intervention—angels and devils are as frequent in their appearances as deities in Homer—but angelic encouragement, and the assistance of his nephew Hoel enables him to rebuild his fleet. He proceeds to win the kingdom in a series of battles in spite of Satan's efforts to destroy him. He finally defeats the Saxon leader in single combat, thus winning the latter's daughter, who has already been promised to him.

King Arthur, the second epic, which appeared two years later, is based on Geoffrey of Monmouth's account of the continental exploits of Arthur, and the source is openly acknowledged.

Much use is made of the *Aeneid*; Spenser's *Faery Queen* may
well be the original of Arthur as paragon of all the virtues. Book
Six, in which Arthur withstands all the horrors and temptations
of Hell's devising, is reminiscent of the Book of Job, but whether
this was consciously used it is hard to say.

As a whole, both poems are entirely modelled on earlier works.
The contest of Raphael and Satan which recurs throughout is
drawn from Milton, much of the heroic adventure from Homer
and Virgil. Political allegory plays a considerable part, and does
not help the tone of the work, since many of the allusions are by
means of contorted name-forms. Although Blackmore achieved
great popularity in his own day, his reputation did not last long.
Several contemporary satires aimed at him, including Pope's
Martin Scriblerus, in which Blackmore is known as Bathos, and
others by Swift and Dryden, were sufficient to destroy this undeserved fame.

It was not for almost a century that Arthur was to reappear in
literature to any extent. Historians of the eighteenth century
reached a view of the historical Arthur not far from that held today, if a little overconfident about dates and places. But it was
not until the antiquarian revival, beginning about the middle of
the century, that any real interest was taken in the Arthur of the
poetic works. Bishop Percy, in his *Reliques of Old English Poetry*,
first published in 1765, included in the final edition of 1794 six or
seven Arthurian poems, debased ballad-forms of earlier works,
and drew attention to many of the romances in a list of his own
compilation. Thomas Warton's *History of English Poetry* contained much general matter on the romances; but the author's
own poems are more interesting to us, for among them are the
only two eighteenth-century ones on Arthur.[2] The first of these,
an ode entitled, *The Grave of King Arthur*, describes the debate
of two bards in front of Henry II as to the whereabouts of
Arthur's grave. The first claims that he was never buried, and
still lives on:

' . . . when he fell, an elfin queen
All in secret and unseen,
O'er the fainting hero threw
Her mantle of ambrosial blue,
And bade her spirits bear him far
In Merlin's agate-axled car
To her green isle's enamelled steep,
Far in the navel of the deep.'

The other denies this, saying that he was buried at Glastonbury:

'In the fair vale of Avalon,
There with chanted orison
And the long blaze of tapers clear
The stolid fathers met the bier;
Through the dim aisles, in order dread
Of martial woe, the chief they led,
And deep intombed in holy ground
Before the solemn altar's bound.'

The other poem, a sonnet in similar vein, is concerned with the Winchester Round Table. Neither is great in poetical standing, but they are interesting as a reflection of the antiquary's knowledge of things Arthurian at this period. Rhetorical in style and rational rather than poetic in approach, their material is drawn from the usual sources, with the addition of Giraldus Cambrensis's account of the Glastonbury burial.

Within a short while editions of the romances proper appeared. Joseph Ritson, whose *Ancient English Metrical Romances* was published in 1802, was one of the more aggressive of the editors He attacks Percy violently for being inaccurate in his reproduction of the original, and follows the manuscripts fastidiously in his own edition. This is of great value to the scholar, but, if carried to extremes, can lead to difficulties for the ordinary reader. He seems to have realized this, and expanded most abbreviations and emended obscure passages where this did not affect the text too severely. This edition was followed by that of *Sir Tristrem* by

Walter Scott, Robert Southey's *Malory*, and Sir F. Madden's *Syr Gawayne*, which collected the majority of the Gawain poems for the first time.

Walter Scott's work is somewhat marred by an excessive admiration for the poet who wrote *Sir Tristrem*, who was no great genius, and certainly not the Thomas of Britain who was then believed to have originated the Tristan and Iseult legend, as Scott so stubbornly maintained. This judgment led him, owing to the importance of the work, to provide his own imitation, which, as such, is very successful. Scott's attitude is best shown by this quotation from a letter written shortly before its publication: 'I am determined not only that my Thomas *shall* be author of *Tristrem*, but also of *Hornchild*.'*

This partisanship in favour of Thomas of Ercildoune appears all the more extraordinary on considering Scott's display of a fairly considerable knowledge of Arthurian literature, at least, for the times, in his one original Arthurian poem. But it must be remembered that this knowledge comes chiefly from the French, and he seems to have been ill acquainted with the English contemporaries of Thomas. This poem, *The Bridal of Triermain*,³ appeared in the *Edinburgh Review* of 1809 without the writer's name, and for some time Scott refused to acknowledge it. He eventually did so, and it is included in his *Collected Works*. It is typical of his style, and seems to have been mainly drawn from his own imagination. The story is a combination of the 'Sleeping Beauty' tale with an Arthurian background, which the first two cantos provide. A brief résumé will convey some idea of the nature of the work.

Arthur is lured from his court by the fairy Guendolen, with whom he spends three years. At the end of this time he leaves her, but has to promise that he will find a husband for their daughter Gyneth when she is of age. In due course, Gyneth arrives at court to claim her due, and a tournament is held to find the knight. At first all is as usual, but later the fighting becomes

* To G. Ellis, 19 March 1804. *Hornchild* is another similar romance.

earnest, and a cousin of Merlin, Vadoc, is killed. Merlin re-
proaches Gyneth for her hardheartedness in not having the fight
stopped, and puts her under a spell by which she will sleep until
a knight finds her and awakes her. The remainder of the poem
concerns the breaking of the spell by Sir Roland de Vaux, many
centuries later.

Scott's main source is revealed by the characters, which come
straight from French romance. Lancelot and Guinevere are
openly lovers: when Gyneth appears and Arthur is forced to
acknowledge her, he glances at Guinevere to see her reaction,
but she simply looks at Lancelot and smiles. Two references to
poems in Percy's *Reliques* show another source of inspiration.
The poem is not of great merit, but is of interest as the only work
by Sir Walter Scott on this subject, and it does mark the real
beginning of the revival of Arthur in literature. He treats the
story in his usual style, familiar from the later novels. Passages
such as this abound:

> 'Now caracoll'd the steeds in air,
> Now plumes and pennons wanton'd fair,
> But soon too earnest grew the game,
> The spears drew blood, the swords struck flame,
> And, horse and man, to ground there came,
> Knights, who shall rise no more!
> Gone was the pride that war had graced,
> Gay shields were cleft, and crests defaced,
> And steel coats riven, and helms unbraced,
> And pennons stream'd with gore.'

Another minor work by a great writer on a similar theme is
even less successful. This is Wordsworth's *The Egyptian Maid*[4]
(1830). It is meant to be a moral tale on the subject of purity, but
neither narrative nor moral stands out clearly. There is no inspiration from the chivalric code, and the poet had certainly read
little other than Malory. Sir Galahad, the only knight never

associated with a lady in the romances, is the husband chosen for the maid, since he is the only one pure enough.

Before embarking on a discussion of the major Arthurian epic of the century, three writers contemporary with Tennyson, but whose works were completed earlier, must be mentioned. The first of these makes use of a tradition that we have so far touched on only briefly, that of Wales. This was to become more widely known after Lady Guest's translation of the *Mabinogi* was published in 1838, but Thomas Love Peacock's novel, *The Misfortunes of Elphin*[5] was written ten years earlier than this. Taliessin appears as Arthur's court poet* and mediator between him and Melwas, King of the Summer Country,† who carries off Guinevere. This is the story told in the eleventh-century *Vita Gildae* of Caradoc of Llancarfan, which we have already had cause to mention.

The whole of Peacock's work has a light and satirical tone; but this disguises an extremely profound knowledge of the subject. He seems to have read almost all the available Welsh literature in the original, and several of the poems are translations from the Welsh. The well-known *War Song of Dinas Vawr* which occurs in this volume, is, however, his own work. Arthur appears only infrequently, but the book is of great interest for its subject matter alone, and is much more entertaining than the rather pompous picture of the Arthurian court presented by the later Victorian writers.

A similarly unusual basis is found in Lord Lytton's *King Arthur*[6] (1848). Arthur is set three tasks in order to secure his kingdom, an idea from Welsh legend. Firstly, he must obtain the sword Excalibur: here the source is Malory. The second task is to get the silver shield of Thor, a borrowing from Norse mythology. Finally, he must visit the Fates, as Perseus visited the Graiae.

Gawain is portrayed here in a more favourable light than

* Cf. the poems of Charles Williams, where he plays the same role.
† This may be Somerset.

L

usual. Lord Lytton, by going back to the earlier stories, including the *Syr Gawayne* collection and some of the French romances, realized and brought out Gawain's original traits of chivalry and humour. Among other incidents, the 'Lit Périlleux' adventure and the incident of the damsel and the brachet* are from the French *Chevalier à l'Épée*. Unfortunately the work as a whole, which could have been very effective and entertaining, is spoilt by the quality of the verse, which tends to be trite, and even in the humorous passages, never harmonizes with the content of the poem.

The story of Tristram and Iseult was to be one of the most popular subjects for the English poets in the next fifty years. The first complete version of the story after that of the thirteenth-century *Sir Tristrem* was written by Matthew Arnold in 1857.[7] His sources were chiefly French, with some use of Malory. Two articles by La Villemarque in the *Revue de Paris*, of 1837, in which a summary of the legend was given, and the similar abbreviation in Dunlop's *History of Prose Fiction* (1842) provided him with the main outline of the story, although he made considerable alterations to both his sources.

The poem is divided into three parts. In the first, Tristram is seen on his death-bed, waiting for Iseult of Ireland to arrive. Unlike the original version, she comes in time to speak to Tristram before his death. The second part is their conversation, a series of memories of the past in which the whole story is reconstructed. Tristram dies, and Iseult of Ireland collapses on his bier. The third and finest part of the poem shows us Iseult of Brittany a year after her husband's death, as she cares for her children.† She tells them the story of Merlin and Vivian, and the poet describes her as she sits alone after they have gone to bed:

* Cf. abstract of *Sir Libeaus Desconus*, Chapter V.
† Again a major departure from the original, where she was Tristtam's wife in name only.

'. . . and then
She'll light her silver lamp, which fishermen
Dragging their nets through the rough waves, afar,
Along this iron coast, know like a star,
And take her broidery-frame, and there she'll sit,
Hour after hour, her gold curls sweeping it;
Lifting her soft-bent head only to mind
Her children, or to listen to the wind.
And when the clock peals midnight, she will move
Her work away, and let her fingers rove
Across the shaggy brows of Tristram's hound
Who lies, guarding her feet, along the ground;
Or else she will fall musing, her blue eyes
Fix'd her slight hands clasp'd on her lap; then rise
And at her prie-dieu kneel, until she have told
The rosary beads of ebony tipp'd with gold;
Then to her soft sleep—and tomorrow'll be
Today's exact repeated effigy.'

The poem is unsuccessful, however, if regarded as a version of
the Tristram and Iseult story. The passion essential to this tale is
never in evidence in Arnold's poem, although it might be argued
that, since the story is unfolded in a series of memories, it is
hardly to be at its full height. If so, the handling of the story is at
fault rather than the actual poetry, for emotion is a necessary
part of any poem on this theme. Another fault is the lack of clear
motivation; we are not sure whether it was preconceived love or
the fatalistic love-potion that was responsible for their tragedy,
and hence we never really understand or sympathize with the
lovers.

Nevertheless, there are some very attractive qualities. It is
Iseult of Brittany who emerges as the real heroine, and the
analysis of her feelings is finely executed, as is description of
lesser details, such as the passage describing Tristram's children
asleep while the lovers talk. Unfortunately the story which

unfolds against this background is not strong enough to bear the weight of the illustrations, and we have a final impression of pictures of incidents of the story rather than a cogent narrative.

We now come to the series of poems, which, after Malory, comprise the best-known English version of the whole Arthurian legend. They are difficult to judge without prejudice, for the reaction against Victorian morals and ideals is not yet complete, and if any one writer embodies all their merits and faults, it is surely Alfred Lord Tennyson.[8]

Before examining in detail the series of poems which make up his Arthurian work, the evolution and general sources will help to make his intentions clearer. Among the memoranda on this subject from his pen is one outlining a single epic poem dated 1833.[9] It sketches the opening of the poem, and runs as follows:

' On the latest limits of the West in the land of Lyonesse, where, save, the rocky isles of Scilly all is now wild sea, rose the sacred Mount of Camelot. It rose from the deeps with gardens and bowers and palaces, and at the top of the Mount was King Arthur's hall, and the holy Minster with the Cross of gold. Here dwelt the King in glory apart, while the Saxons whom he had overthrown in twelve battles ravaged the land, and ever came nearer and nearer.

' The Mount was the most beautiful in the world, sometimes green and fresh in the beam of morning, sometimes all one splendour, folded in the golden mists of the West. But all underneath it was hollow, and the mountain trembled when the seas rushed bellowing through the porphyry caves; and there ran a prophecy that the mountain and the city on some wild morning would topple into the abyss and be no more.

' It was night. The King sat in his Hall. Beside him sat the sumptuous Guinevere and about him were all his lords and knights of the Table Round. There they feasted, and when the feast was over the bards sang to the King's glory.'

Although the reviews of his 1842 volume of poetry deterred him from carrying out this plan, a second memoir gives an outline of the underlying symbolism, and this is some indication of the ideas on which the whole scheme of Tennyson's cycle is based. King Arthur himself was to represent religious faith, and was to have two wives, the first of whom was to be banished before he married the second, but later recalled. They were both to be called Guinevere,* the first being the symbol of primitive Christianity, the second of Roman Catholicism. Mordred represented scepticism and Merlin science; Merlin's daughter was to wed Mordred. The Lady of the Lake, Nimue, stands for evil and corruption, a role which was little altered in the final version. Among the objects attached to Arthur, Excalibur was to be war, and the Round Table 'liberal institutions'.

Little of this formidable religious symbolism was directly adopted in the *Idylls of the King*, but it cannot altogether have passed from Tennyson's mind. Dating from some years later, there is a draft outlining a masque to be written on the Arthurian legends. Chronology and general appearance of the legend are much altered; it is difficult to imagine the possible result:

FIRST ACT: Sir Mordred and his party. Mordred inveighs against the King and the Round Table. The knights, and the quest. Mordred scoffs at the Ladies of the Lake, doubts whether they are supernatural beings, etc. Mordred's cringing interview with Guinevere. Mordred and the Lady of the Lake. Arthur lands in Albyn.

SECOND ACT: Lancelot's embassy and Guinevere. The Lady of the Lake meets Arthur and endeavours to persuade him not to fight with Sir Mordred. Arthur will not be moved from his purpose. Lamentation of the Lady of the Lake. Elaine. Marriage of Arthur.

THIRD ACT: Oak tomb of Merlin. The song of Nimue.

* The idea of the true and false Guinevere occurs in Welsh legend, and also in the fourteenth-century English romance *Arthour and Merlin* (q.v.).

Sir Mordred comes to consult Merlin. Coming away meets
Arthur. Their fierce dialogue. Arthur consults Sir L. and
Sir Bedivere. Arthur weeps over Merlin and is reproved by
Nimue, who inveighs against Merlin. Arthur asks Merlin
the issue of the battle. Merlin will not enlighten him. Nimue
requests Arthur to question Merlin again. Merlin tells him he
shall bear rule again, but that the Ladies of the Lake can
return no more. Guinevere throws away the diamonds into
the river. The Court and the dead Elaine.

FOURTH ACT: Discovery by Merlin and Nimue of Lancelot and Guinevere. Arthur and Guinevere's meeting and
parting.

FIFTH ACT: The battle. Chorus of the Ladies of the Lake.
The throwing away of Excalibur and departure of Arthur.

Tennyson did not finally decide on even the general shape of
the cycle until some ten years later, in about 1855. After this,
work progressed much more rapidly. He had in the interval read
much of the earlier Arthurian literature, including Malory, of
whose *Morte Darthur* there had been three editions between
1816 and 1821, and who was now generally known, the *Mabinogion*, in the original Welsh and in Lady Guest's translation of
1838, *Layamon*, and some of the French romances. From this
material he shaped his versions of the legends.

The symbolism and ideal underlying the final work seems to
have been altered slightly and continuously as he progressed—
unlike Malory, who, having found the ideal hero, proceeded to
work everything out to this preconceived ideal. Nor can Tennyson's symbolism be too literally interpreted. He said on one
occasion: 'I hate to be tied down to say, "This means that", because the thought within the image is much more than any one
interpretation.' Yet on another occasion he provides a seemingly
contradictory indication: 'Of course Camelot for instance . . . is
everywhere symbolic of the gradual growth of human beliefs and
institutions, and of the spiritual development of man. Yet there

is no single fact in the *Idylls*, however seemingly mystical, which cannot be explained without any mystery or allegory whatsoever.' His final judgment seems to have been this: 'Poetry is like shot-silk with many glancing colours. Every reader must find his own interpretation according to his ability, and according to his sympathy with the poet.'

From these three statements we can gather that a broad general symbolism, which must not be worked out to its ultimate conclusion, was intended. Arthur stands for the ideal soul: the story is that of man's Utopian dreams coming into contact with practical life and the warring elements of the flesh, and being ruined by one sin. Arthur's birth is a mystery, as is his death: between the two lies Life with its conflict of flesh and spirit. He attempts to realize himself in the world of sense, represented by Guinevere, and to control and elevate human passion and capacity by 'liberal institutions' (the Round Table).* Thus Sir Galahad, who might at first seem to be the hero of the poems, is not in fact Tennyson's ideal: he is the figure of spiritual life divorced from this earth, who negates man's dual nature by withdrawing into purely spiritual realms. Merlin is the intellect, and his disastrous affair with Vivian is symbolic of the corruption of the intellectual by the sensual.

There is a unified progression towards the conclusion which is reflected by the extent to which the sin of Lancelot and Guinevere corrupts the court. We find Balin unable to save himself because of the false ideals they have spread: Pelleas and Etarre imitate their sin: the Holy Grail is misunderstood and misused by the knights imbued by this worldly ideal, of whom Lancelot is the chief, and they approach it with superstition instead of reverence. *The Last Tournament* shows the final stage of this process, cynicism. This poem was originally entitled *The True and the False*, and indeed it contrasts the decay caused by the false ideal with the original truth. Lancelot the bold has become

---

* This is one of the few points of the symbolic draft retained in the later version without any alteration.

inactive, Tristram the courteous has forgotten his courtesy. Yet Tennyson does not leave the ending of the cycle without a ray of hope. There is the way of repentance taken by Lancelot and Guinevere, and the forgiveness offered to them by Arthur. The final passage of the *Passing of Arthur* is on a note of hope.

Another linking theme which gives the poems a further unity is that of the changing seasons. *The Coming of Arthur* takes place on New Year's Day. His wedding is 'when the world is white with may'. The Grail appears at Camelot on a summer's night. *The Last Tournament* is in autumn, and the final battle at midwinter. The whole cycle is thus represented as one natural year.

There are few difficulties in the poems themselves, but the first, *The Coming of Arthur*, is one of the more obscure. Tennyson, not wishing to retain the earlier version of the story of Arthur's birth, in his view immoral and unsuited to the conception of Arthur as ideal man, shrouds this event in mystery, and no definite facts are allowed to emerge. The question of his origin arises out of King Leodegrance's wish to know more about him before giving him his daughter Guinevere in marriage. This explains why the question of birth predominates this account of his early career rather than the usual twelve battles against the Saxons.

Gareth and Lynette is a straightforward paraphrase of Malory's *Book of Gareth*, but for the two Geraint poems, Tennyson turned to the *Mabinogion*. The original of the Welsh is the source of Chrétien de Troyes's *Erec et Enide*. Enid becomes the Victorian ideal wife, a sort of Patient Griselda, just as she had earlier been the ideal of chivalric womanhood. The song 'Turn, fortune, turn thy wheel and lower the proud', was probably inspired by Arthur's dream of fortune's wheel in Layamon. Malory is again the source for the next two poems, *Balin and Balan*,[10] and *Merlin and Vivien*.[11] Balin, however, is not merely a fated knight, but is unable to redeem himself because of the corruption at court. Vivien is in Malory and in Tennyson's first sketches known as Nimue, the Lady of the Lake; but the French romances use the

former name, and it is hence the earlier of the two. Broceliande
is based on the New Forest, which he visited on one of his
autumn tours. Salisbury and Amesbury were also included on
such tours to enable the poet to recreate the atmosphere of
medieval towns.

Lancelot and Elaine offers a very striking contrast between
Tennyson's and Malory's approach, but is otherwise straightforward. An example of this contrast may be quoted:

> '. . . lay the letter in my hand,
> A little ere I die, and close the hand
> Upon it; I shall guard it even in death,
> And when the heat is gone out from my heart
> Then take the little bed on which I died
> For Lancelot's love, and deck it like the Queen's
> For richness, and me also like the Queen
> In all I have of rich, and lay me on it.
> And let there be prepared a chariot-bier
> To take me to the river, and a barge
> Be ready on the river, clothed in black.
> I go in state to court, to meet the Queen.
> There surely shall I speak for mine own self,
> And none of you can speak for me so well.
> And therefore let our dumb old man alone
> Go with me, he can steer and row, and he
> Will guide me to that palace, to the doors.'

'And whyle my body ys hote lat thys lettir be put in my
ryght honde, and my honde bounde fasté to the letter untyll
that I be colde. And lette me be put in a fayre bed with all
the rychyste clothys that I have aboute me, and so lat my
bed and all my rychyst clothis be ledde with me in a charyat
unto the nexte place where the Temmys ys; and there lette
me be put within a barget, and but one man with me, such
as ye truste, to stirre me thidir; and that my barget be

coverde with blacke samyte over and over. And thus, fadir,
I beseche you, lat hit be done.'

Malory's own *Tale of the Sankgreall* receives much the same
treatment as that which the writer gave to the French romances.
Tennyson extracts various incidents and welds them into a very
compact and unified whole. The alteration in symbolism has
already been discussed: the real difference is that Malory had
little respect for the 'celestial' chivalry of the *Queste del Saint
Graal*, and did not hesitate to show it, whereas Tennyson, while
disliking the idea of isolation of the spirit from the flesh, could
only relegate it to a secondary motif, and leave his own opinion
undefined. His attitude towards Lancelot clashes most violently
with Malory's at this point, and his condemnation of him is far
stronger than that of any other writer.

To illustrate the decay of the court, Tennyson ignores the sequence of the *Morte Darthur*, which so far has been approximately followed, and takes the incident of Pelleas and Etarre
from Book IV.[12] He has altered this story little, save that Pelleas
blames Lancelot and Guinevere for his plight, and finds no con-
solation with Nimue. *The Last Tournament* is a compilation of
various incidents scattered through Malory, Dagonet's part being
Tennyson's own contribution. It is here that Tristram appears
for the only time, naturally in a somewhat unfavourable light.

Guinevere again disregards the old chronology, for in all other
writers, the Queen's retirement to a convent had taken place
after the last battle, and not before; her stay there is usually said
to have lasted seven years. This poem was at one point intended
as the final unit of the cycle, which probably explains this.
Tennyson did not feel that he could improve on Arthur's speech
as an ending, but he eventually realized that the *Morte D'Arthur*
of the 1842 collection, based on the last book of Malory,[13] could
well be adapted to provide a less static finale, and he accordingly
added 169 lines at the beginning* describing Arthur's dream and

---

* From the beginning to 'So all day long the battle roll'd'.

the actual battle, putting in several references to give it coherence with the rest of the cycle. In the final twenty-nine lines, also added at this time, in which Bedivere's last actions are portrayed, we find the riddle given by Merlin in the *Coming of Arthur*, or at least its refrain, which has occurred elsewhere in the poem: 'From the great deep to the great deep he goes', symbolizing Arthur's mysterious birth and death.

We have already contrasted Tennyson's style with that of Malory, and a few further remarks may not be out of place. The earlier poems are in a form akin to the ballad, which, although effective, is less suitable for sustained work. However, the later parts of the cycle are in a less rhythmical verse-form. To the modern reader, the descriptions may well seem better than the characterization and psychology, possibly because his moralizing is not popular today. It may also be because character in his main source, Malory, is based on a code which was unacceptable to him, and he failed to remould the heroes without losing this character. His failure to create new characters is due to his approach to the work, which he saw as a vehicle for his ideas rather than as an end in itself. Neither Lancelot nor Guinevere is convincing, even if the scene between the latter and the novice in the monastery does reveal some human traits. Like so many ideal heroes, Arthur is unreal; his perfection tends to be in-human, and Tennyson narrowly escapes making him intolerably aloof. Of the minor characters, the distraught Pelleas is lifelike, and the simple Elaine is well-drawn. Few of the others have any interest beyond their actual part in the plot.

It is hard for us today to recapture Tennyson's original im-pact, so debased has his noble idiom become through imitation and too frequent quotation. If he seems on occasions to lack real feeling, there is always an atmosphere of high purpose in the tone of the poetry. It was this nobility that was dearest to his heart, a virtue too old-fashioned to be appreciated now. Chivalry is exalted over passion, the rational conclusion of the trend started in Malory, and which enables him to give a more unified account of the legend because he is free to omit the Tristram episodes, that part of the stories which disturbs most the continuity of Malory's eight tales. Even if we cannot entirely sympathize with the moral tone of the work as its first readers did, there are many individual passages which are in themselves among the finest of English poetry.

In very different mood are the Arthurian poems of William Morris.[14] We have similarly an early sketch for an Arthurian epic, fragments of which include *The Maying of Queen Guinevere*, *Sir Palomides' Quest*, *Iseult of Brittany*, and a descriptive opening to *The Defence of Guinevere*. None of these is in itself of interest, but they can help to clarify the four Arthurian poems included in his *Collected Works*.

The Defence of Guenevere is the Queen's speech defending herself at her trial. Lancelot's and Guinevere's love is vague and indecisive: we never know whether they are in fact in the least guilty, though the repeated refrain

> 'Nevertheless, you, O sir Gauwaine, lie,
> Whatever may have happen'd these long years,
> God knows I speak truth, saying that you lie!'

scarcely carries conviction, and there seems to be admission of guilt in several places. It may be that a difference between guilt in the eyes of God and in the opinion of earthly judges is implied. As far as there is any particular source, Malory is used. *King Arthur's Tomb* is more successful. The impenitent Guinevere is beautifully drawn, and there is strength and colour in the images evoked. But the ending is again inconclusive, and the poem as a whole suffers from being too much a picture and too little a narrative.

Sir Galahad likewise has a poor plot, but the idea of temptation and a certain amount of atmosphere are conveyed. The intention seems to be confused, and there is a lack of conviction about the angels. The last of the group, *The Chapel in Lyonesse* is obscure in meaning and origin. Sir Galahad appears to be in fact the totally different Sir Galyhud of Malory, who accompanies Bors and Lancelot to the chapel where Arthur is buried. Ozanna le Cure Hardy is very unobtrusive, being one of the knights who accompany Guinevere on her maying expedition.[15] Whether this association led Morris to substitute him for Lancelot is hard to tell. The only alternative is to regard the incident as entirely invented. It is the most beautiful of the four poems.

This group is ample evidence that the proposed cycle would have been beyond Morris's capacity. His power lies in the evocation of a single event or image: thus the last poem's brevity makes it effective, while the first is much longer and fails to hold the attention. His object was the realization of a tragic event or situation 'the perception and experience of tragic truth, of subtle and noble, terrible and piteous things'; nor is there in this almost visionary sight much order or composing of ideas. But the pictures remain for us to enjoy, firm in mood and setting if we do not look for the usual requisites in character and plot.

Morris's Arthurian poems are irrelevant to his fame: but the same is by no means true of Algernon Swinburne.[16] *Tristram of Lyonesse* was always intended to be, and is, his magnum opus. It is the finest of the English poems on this subject, and covers most of the events of the legend; Swinburne seems to have tried to gain the maximum poetic effect from each passage, and the result is rich but a little overweighted.

Much reading preceded the composition of this poem. Swinburne has studied the earliest of the romances, those of Thomas of Britain and Béroul, as far as they were known, as well as *Sir Tristrem* and Scott's continuation of it, and Malory. The result is a story that rarely departs from the earliest form, save in the Palomides and Joyous Gard episodes, but which omits some of the excessive detail and hence has a generally simpler outline.

The poem gains greatly from a clear motive force, that of passionate love. Tennyson had condemned this love fiercely; Swinburne as fiercely glorifies it, yet is aware of its sinful nature.

He takes a similar though more lenient view to that of Dante, who placed it in the *Inferno*, yet only as one of the lesser sins, since it involves mutual sacrifice even if it acknowledges no loyalty outside itself, and hence leads the participants to betray others. Swinburne excuses this last trait to some extent by his characterization of Mark as mean and cold-blooded, until it is time for him to offer them noble forgiveness in death, and, having learnt the whole story, to speak the moving epilogue.

As a story pure and simple, it is obscured by psychological excursions, protracted similes, and lengthy description. But to take it as a mere telling of the tragedy would be to miss all its poetic qualities. It is rather a continuous evocation of their feelings as this tragedy progresses: from the amazement of their first fiery kiss through the woes of separation and joys of reunion, to the last moving scene where the young and spirited lovers are finally revealed as grown old and subject to death.

Theme and motif are highly important to the unity of the story: the first and last embraces connected by the same words repeated with variation:

'Their heads neared, and their hands were drawn in one,
And they saw dark, though still the unsunken sun
Far through fine rain shot fire into the south;
And their four lips became one burning mouth.'

'. . . and her head
Bowed, as to reach the spring that slakes all drouth;
And their four lips became one silent mouth.'

This is but the most striking of many examples. Another is provided by the names of the ships: 'Swallow' bears Tristram on the first fateful voyage, and 'Swan' carries Iseult on her last journey to Tristram. One theme runs throughout the whole poem, pervading it and occasionally dominating the verse: the sea itself. Both for Malory and the unknown author of *Sir Tristrem*, the hero had been a knight of the greenwood, a hunter

skilled in venery. But for the earliest romancers and for those
before them who had formed and shaped the heart of the legend,
Tristram was essentially a man of the sea. Swinburne's realization of this has provided him with a powerful and closely connected background against which to set his poem which claims
almost as much of his verse as the story itself. *Iseult at Tintagel*,
which shows her in separation thinking of her lover, is continually
underlined by the mood of the sea. The most famous lines,
which sum up the part of the sea in the poem, are these:

> 'And all their past came wailing in the wind,
> And all their future thundered in the sea.'

The sea sets off and heightens the great moments of the tragedy.
The famous love-potion is drunk against a background of storm;
Tristram and Iseult look seawards for comfort when they are
parted; the lovelessness of Tristram's marriage to Iseult of the
White Hands is emphasized by the sea's absence, and the
one moment of calm at Joyous Gard is mirrored in the sea's
mood:

> 'Nor loved they life for death's sake less,
> Nor feared they death for love's or life's sake more
> And on the sounding soft funereal shore
> They, watching till the day should wholly die,
> Saw the far sea sweep to the far grey sky,
> Saw the long sands sweep to the long grey sea.
> And night made one sweet mist of moor and lea,
> And only far off shore the foam gave light.
> And life in them sank silent as the night.'

The psychology of such love is drawn with amazing skill. Never
do we feel unreality or contradiction in their actions or feelings.
Tristram's attitude to Iseult of Brittany is beautifully analysed,
as are her feelings when he deserts her. Tristram's death, a
difficult subject on which to avoid bathos, is well handled. The
jealous Iseult of Brittany, who has accidentally learnt of the

prearranged signal, tells him that the sail is black, which means that her namesake of Ireland is not coming:

> 'And fain he would have sprung upright and seen,
> And spoken; but strong death struck sheer between . . .'

Such unrestrained passion as this story involves becomes all too easily trite or ridiculous, but Swinburne's poetry never suffers from either of these faults. The work as a whole may well be compared to a richer and more poetic version of Chrétien de Troyes. The same psychological detail, the same secondary regard for narrative, the same lifelike portraits, are but a few of the traits that are reminiscent of the latter. Nor is *Tristram of Lyonesse* any less a great work of art.

Swinburne's other Arthurian work, *The Tale of Balen*, is in many ways as effective as *Tristram of Lyonesse*, and gains from a more compact, less diffuse, style. It lacks, however, the sheer power of poetry, and the driving motive of love, which cannot be equalled by that of Fate. The story, taken from Malory, is written in verse reminiscent of medieval stanzaic romance, just as *Tristram of Lyonesse* has affinities with the alliterative verse of the same period. This association is strengthened by the inclusion of the stanzas on nature at the beginning of Cantos I, II, VI, and VII. Like the *Idylls of the King*, the action takes place within one natural year. Balen's youth is described against a background of spring. The battle that marks the height of his fame is in summer, but autumn brings approaching doom, and winter, death. For some of the settings, Swinburne was inspired by the Northumberland of his youth, although the poem was written at the end of his life.

The story itself in Malory is one of pathos rather than tragedy. Balen's slaying of his brother is more of an accident than a fore-ordained doom. The latter view is Swinburne's, and this is his major alteration in the poem, for it arises from Balen's refusal to return a sword when asked to do so, and hence there is a definite chain of cause and effect. But this is contradicted by the feeling of the poem, which ignores the fact that it is Balen's own fault, and thus gains more from the tragic effect.

The simplicity and directness remarked on previously is achieved by the absence of any abstract philosophizing; this last is by no means lacking in *Tristram of Lyonesse*. It is replaced by images and similes from nature against which the action takes place, as for example the use of the natural year as a framework to the poem.

After Tennyson's enormous success, a host of lesser writers seized eagerly upon the Arthurian stories, and it would be a vain and not in the least rewarding task to assess each of their efforts. A few may be mentioned here, especially those who have treated the material in an original or effective way.

R. S. Hawker,[17] the Cornish antiquary whom Tennyson visited on one of his tours, composed a *Quest of the Sangreal* which is unexpectedly independent of the other poet's work. His use of unusual sources, chiefly continental, is an interesting feature of his poem, although he relies in the main on Malory. Hebrew words are mixed with Cornish names and strange expressions in a way that is somehow reminiscent of Thomas Love Peacock, while the medieval and mystic tone of his work is almost diametrically opposed to that of *The Misfortunes of Elphin*.

The Holy Grail is also the theme of two other largely original poems. One, by J. R. Lowell,[18] the American poet, is a protest against what is, in the author's opinion the selfish attitude found towards the Grail in most works. Sir Launfal, the hero of the title, is about to set out in quest of it, but is shown in a dream that its achievement really lies in helping others, which can best be done at home.

The Last Ballad, by John Davidson,[19] is a rearrangement of various events in Lancelot's life to fit in with the poet's ideas. Here Guinevere becomes Lancelot's ideal and hence his personal Grail. This conception was intimately connected with the

M

poet's own philosophy of life. It does portray the neglected spiritual side of Lancelot and Guinevere's love, and as such is successful.

The remaining writers are playwrights. Arthurian material has not as a whole been successfully dramatized, least of all Tennyson's idea of it, although plays based on his works did have a temporary success when presented in London. It requires a skill and nobility of expression not possessed by most writers who have attempted it, if such work is to avoid the banal. We have yet to see a really great Arthurian drama in English; the best attempt yet is probably Masefield's *Tristan and Isolt*, which belongs to our next chapter.

Richard Hovey's *Lancelot and Guinevere* (1891)[20] lacks the vital quality of dignity, and deliberate 'humanization' of the story takes place, with the result that their love is debased into a mere intrigue against Arthur. J. Comyns Carr produced two plays on Arthurian themes, *King Arthur* (1896) and *Tristram and Iseult* (1906), neither of which rises above the average. In the latter, alteration of the story detracts from its tragic force. Mark is jealous of Tristram from the beginning, and hence the conflict between Tristram's friendship for Mark and his love for Iseult is non-existent, and the situation loses dramatic value by being simplified.

Under the pseudonym of 'Michael Field', Katharine Bradley and Edith Cooper produced two plays on Tristram and Iseult, *The Tragedy of Pardon* (1911) and *Tristan de Leonois* (1913). The story as told by Thomas of Britain is the basis for both. Neither has any great qualities: the first suffers from a lack of decisive character and sometimes of dignity, and the incidents chosen are scarcely suited to the stage, among them the substitution of Brangwain, Iseult's handmaid, for her mistress on Mark's wedding night, and the latter's discovery of the lovers sleeping with a sword between them. In *Tristan de Leonois* the magical element, especially that connected with the love-potion, is over-emphasized.

A basis of the German medieval poem "Tristan" by Gottfried of Strassburg, and Richard Wagner's libretto for his own
opera, was used in Arthur Symons's *Tristram and Iseult* (1917).
It opens with Tristram's second visit to Ireland, to fetch Iseult
for Mark. The latter is portrayed as an old man, thus making
their love more natural, and the duel that of love and loyalty.
When their love is discovered, Iseult becomes the dominant
character, declaring her freedom to love, whereas Tristram remains bound by his honour, and refuses to use the magic
draught as an excuse. But Mark, on hearing of the love-potion
after their death, expresses deep sorrow at not having learnt of
it earlier, as in Swinburne.

There is an effective fatalistic atmosphere. Iseult is the more
determined of the lovers, for Tristram fears the implications of
their love. Its first ecstasy does not sustain him in later trouble.
Although this portrayal of love's bitterness and frustration is a
legitimate view of the situation, it makes a pathetic rather than
tragic figure of Tristram. It is Iseult's flame that devours Tristram, instead of a mutual kindling of love; she almost says as
much as she mourns over his body:

> 'This dust was a fire and burned the stars:
> Now what little ashes holds the fire
> That was blown out too early. There is nothing
> Left in the world, and I am out of place.'

Symons's play has moments of great power, yet never sustains
its promise of a really good stage version of the legend.

In the four centuries just discussed, a far greater change came
over Arthurian literature and the attitude to the historical Arthur
than in the similar period preceding them. From a dying romance
literature sprang rationalism and the more classical type of epic.
But it was the scholars who were also responsible for the revival
of interest at the beginning of the nineteenth century, and the
greater appreciation of such works since then is in some measure

due to their rediscovery of earlier versions. The poetic possibilities of the legends were once again realized, but usually with a new purpose behind them. It is the exception rather than the rule to find a Victorian portrait of Arthur without any moral attached to him, and it is this that makes so many of the efforts of this period second-rate, the moral getting more attention than anything else in the poem. Yet none the less the greatest telling of the legends in recent days is founded on this principle. When it is remembered that the major facet of the cycle lacking in the *Idylls of the King* is more than adequately made up by *Tristram of Lyonesse*, the nineteenth century may well be called the heyday of Arthur as a figure of English literature.

NINE

THE MODERN VIEW

THE last fifty years have seen a more diverse approach to Arthurian literature than any previous period. The tendency of the Victorian writers to regard the legends as material for moral illustration rather than as a great tale requiring skill in the telling has already been pointed out. The modern writers, with one notable exception, have returned to the latter view, but have used widely differing methods.

Some of the minor writers of the early twentieth century have been discussed in the previous essay, chiefly those whose style and attitude connected them with the Victorian era. Laurence Binyon's poem, *Tristram's End* (1913),[1] although their contemporary, shows a more modern approach and is more poetically conceived and executed than any of the other minor versions of the Tristram legend mentioned there. It is a close study of character as revealed by the stresses of the final scenes of the story.

The events of the story are barely mentioned, and a full appreciation of the poem requires a knowledge of the details. As the poem opens, Tristram is on his deathbed; but when the incident of the sail occurs, he gets up, and sees that it is white, and not, as Iseult of the White Hands had said, black. Iseult of Ireland reaches him before he dies, and after a long last farewell, in which they remember incidents of their past life and love, they find death in each other's arms.

The atmosphere is very different from that in *Tristram of Lyonesse*; here there is quiet regret and looking back to past joys and sorrows whose keen edges have been blunted by time. The violent jealousy of Iseult of Brittany turns to remorse at her husband's death, and we see that she too had loved him in her own way:

> 'I loved him not enough, I could not keep
> His heart, and yet I loved him, o how deep!
> I cannot touch him. Will none set him free
> From those arms and give him me?'

Similarly, Mark expresses his love for Iseult over her bier, calm and composed, yet with the same strain of regret in his voice:

> 'Iseult, I would have fenced thee from men's sight,
> My treasure, that I found so very fair,
> The treasure I had taken with a snare:
> To keep thee mine, this was my life's delight.
> And now the end is come, alone I stand,
> And the hand that lies in thine is not my hand.'

The love-potion is relegated to a minor position as cause of their love. Tristram expresses his thankfulness that it was through no 'wizard wine' that he came to love her, but through a love that had already sprung up. He regrets having kept his word to King Mark and given Iseult to him. The sea-influence is strong throughout.

The poem, although restricted in scope, is very effective, as great as an expression of the atmosphere of Tristram's death as any other. It does not set out to tell the story in a series of remembered pictures, but to portray its closing scene, which it does swiftly and energetically. This compression is very much to the work's advantage.

Thomas Hardy's play, *The Famous Tragedy of the Queen of Cornwall* (1923)[2] presents us with a very different and more active version of Tristram's death. He combines the two traditions of Malory and the early writers: the episode of the black and white sails precedes the opening of the play, and Tristram and Iseult have merely fallen into a trance, and have not seen each other. Tristram then sets off to Cornwall in pursuit of her, and it is here that the scene of the play is placed. In the action of the play, Malory is followed, and it is Mark who kills Tristram. Iseult's killing of Mark and suicide are Hardy's own invention, as is Iseult of Brittany's appeal to the Cornish queen to come and heal Tristram, which has already taken place before the play starts.

The structure of the play itself is unusual, and is reminiscent of Greek tragedy. Two choruses, male and female, are used to comment on and explain the action. Merlin speaks a Prologue and Epilogue. This external addition does not always help the play, and fails entirely to fill in the necessary background, but often lends weight to the action.

The style of the play is at once its weakest and strongest point. A use of unusual and archaic words tends to be distracting and harsh on the ear: 'thrid' and 'glode' are examples. Yet some of the lyrical outbursts are among Hardy's best poetry. He mingles to too great an extent the commonplace and the poetic: 'King Howel's lass of Brittany' is scarcely an apt description of Iseult of the White Hands as she appears later in the play.

Of the characters, Mark and Andret—as in Malory—are the villains: the former has no redeeming traits whatsoever. Rough, boorish and treacherous, it is he who actually kills Tristram. Iseult of the White Hands is therefore completely exonerated from any responsibility for Tristram's death. She is jealous, but not to excess; and in many ways she seems the most human character in the play. The lovers themselves are unevenly portrayed, and fail to make much impression.

It is the same unevenness of approach and hence of the tone of the poetry that mars the play: Hardy seems to have been uncertain as to what extent it should be the 'mummery-play' of the stage directions, and how far it should be the 'Famous Tragedy' of the title. Had he been consistent in his handling of the theme, we might well have had a major Arthurian drama from his hand, but as it stands the play is only a partial success.

T. S. Eliot's *The Waste Land* may be a landmark of English literature, but for us it is interesting in that it has as a basis a critical work on Arthurian literature, Miss J. L. Weston's *From Ritual to Romance*, in which her theories on the origins of the Grail are outlined. Yet it is in some ways unfortunate that the poet should have chosen this book, for, exciting though her theories are, they are now regarded as inaccurate. But on the other hand, *The Waste Land* is only connected to this specific work by the symbolism of spear and cup in the two, and as for all other Arthurian references, any outline of the legend will be sufficient to elucidate them: the poem is only incidentally Arthurian, in spite of its title.

Yet another version of the Tristram legend comes from the pen of an American writer. E. A. Robinson's *Tristram* (1928),[3] awarded the Pulitzer Prize for that year, is the first real success in Arthurian literature from the other side of the Atlantic. It is more in the tradition of Arnold than Swinburne, and there is further a sceptical rationalism in his revision of the story. The love-potion is entirely absent, and the lovers die by Andret's hand. As in Symons, the tendency is not to portray the ecstasy of passionate love, but the resulting torment:

> 'And for a time nothing was to be heard
> Except the pounding of two hearts in prison,
> The torture of a doom-begotten music
> Above them, and the wash of a cold foam
> Below them on those cold eternal rocks
> Where Tristram and Iseult had yesterday
> Come to be wrecked together. When her eyes
> Opened again, he saw there, watching him,
> An aching light of memory; and his heart beat
> Beat harder for remembering the same light
> That he had seen before in the same eyes.'

It is Tristram who seems to be compelled to torture himself, whereas Iseult is more determined and clear-headed, and appears to realize the presence of

'. . . Fate, that like an unseen ogre
Made hungry sport of these two there alone
Above the moaning wash of Cornish water,
Cold upon the Cornish rocks.'

This is no serene security in a requited love, but a reflection of the neuroses which seem to typify love to so many modern poets. Iseult of Brittany, however, is the poet's real favourite. Her calm stoicism in Tristram's absence is nearest to Robinson's own attitude to life, and her quiet watching for him, even after she has learnt of his death, forms the closing scene of the poem:

'Isolt of the white hands,
Isolt with her grey eyes and her white face,
Still gazed across the water for the north
But not now for a ship . . .
                    '. . . Yet there she gazed
Across the water, over the white waves,
Upon a castle that she had never seen,
And would not see, save as a phantom shape
Against a phantom sky. He had been there,
She thought, but not with her. He had died there,
But not for her. He had not thought of her,
Perhaps, and that was strange. He had been all,
And would be always all there was for her,
And he had not come back to her alive,
Not even to go again.'

The language and the effect of blank verse is at first strange, but essentially clear and poetical. *Tristram* is the best American contribution to the legend yet.

John Masefield's *Midsummer Night and other tales in verse* (1927)[4] presents us with a series of linked pictures and incidents that cover the main events of the life of Arthur. Much new and unfamiliar material is introduced, and the legends are freely altered. These poems have received less attention than they deserve, and a brief examination of them separately will help to illustrate the poet's methods and clarify some of his more obscure sources.

The poems can be divided into eight groups, of which the first deals with Arthur's birth. The first poem, *The Begetting of Arthur*, is the most radical departure from tradition. Uther comes to Merchyon of Cornwall on a political mission, and sees his daughter Ygerne, with whom he falls in love. The same night he elopes with her in disguise, having failed both in his original mission and in his attempt to get her father's permission to marry her. They go just beyond the borders of Merchyon's land, and rest for the night in a grove. Here Merchyon overtakes them; he stabs the sleeping Uther, and takes Ygerne back to Tintagel, where she bears Arthur. This attractive story seems to be entirely of the poet's own invention, as is the next poem, although this latter is reminiscent of the fairy elements in Layamon's story. It describes how, soon after Arthur is born, Ygerne takes him to a magical stone chair by the sea-shore, on which she lays him. A procession of those who will be associated with him in later life appear, including his mysterious 'Helper', each foretelling his part.

The beginnings of tragedy are laid in the next two poems, *The Taking of Morgause* and *The Begetting of Mordred*. Morgause, Ygerne's sister, is captured by Lot of Orkney and his pirates. She becomes his queen, and arrives at Arthur's court as a spy; but although 'love was between them for one summer's night' she cannot find out anything from Arthur about the wars that are imminent.

Badon Hill marks the climax of Arthur's career. The story is straightforward: Arthur's great enemies, the Saxon pirates, make a raid far up the rivers into the downlands of the West: they fail to find any cattle, and as they drink and play dice in their camp,

Arthur and Lancelot burn their ships. In the great battle that ensues, he slaughters them all.

Masefield now turns to three already established but little-known legends. Two are Arthurian, the third completely strange to Arthur. The basis of *The Sailing of Hell Race* is the poem *The Spoils of Annwfn*, one of the few surviving Welsh fragments.* The mysterious voyage from which only Arthur and seven warriors return is elaborated by Masefield. Here the three kingdoms of Hell are visited—the first of Lady Self and Mammon, the second of War, and finally that of Sloth and Pestilence. The first two are safely passed, but only the intervention of his Helper saves him from the clutches of the third. On his return he meets Guinevere, and the next poem, *Arthur and his Ring* follows on immediately. The story is that of Venus and the ring, taken from classical writers. A lover slips his beloved's ring on to the hand of a statue of Venus, and has to beg it from the goddess herself in order to get it off again. She offers him eternal life if he will stay with her, but he prefers his beloved and death.

With the appearance of Guinevere, the characters of the final tragedy are now complete, and *Midsummer Night*, the title-poem, shows how each was to blame. The poet uses the old legend that Arthur is sleeping in a cave,[5] and awakens every Midsummer Night. He accidentally finds the way to this cave, and hears the various characters tell how they contributed to the catastrophe. Gwenivach, Guinevere's sister and Mordred's wife, is found in Welsh legend, and Masefield includes her here. Each in turn blames himself or herself alone; all save Mordred regret what they have done. The truth is that all have played a part, and all are responsible. Arthur then prophesies his return, and they vanish.

The last group of poems unfolds the actual events of the tragedy, and falls into three parts. The first deals with the breaking-up of Arthur's company of knights. Mordred's surprising of Lancelot and Guinevere is taken from Malory, and the

* See Chapter 3.

spirit of revenge predominates over justice in the attitude of the twelve knights. Lancelot fights them each in turn on the narrow parapet of the wall; a dramatic touch is lent by the insight into the thoughts of each knight as he falls to his death. Mordred alone escapes, and demands justice from Arthur. *The Breaking of the Links* tells how Lancelot's comrades remained faithful to him, and Arthur, in consenting to Mordred, drives them into open opposition. However, a new pirate invasion causes Mordred and Arthur to form an alliance, and the King departs, hoping that this new combination will prove as strong as the old.

But this hope is vain: in *Gwenivach Tells*, Mordred's wife explains why at her instigation Mordred allied himself with the invading pirates, thus leading to the final stage of the tragedy. Arthur's hesitancy to fight against his son is described in *Arthur in the Ruins*. His Helper appears and tells him that this is his appointed destiny, giving him a token to show that this is true. Nevertheless, he tries to arbitrate before the battle, which is related by the last two poems. Kolgrim the pirate grows tired of talking, and tries to assassinate Arthur. The attempt fails, and battle is joined. Neither side prevails until Lancelot arrives with cavalry and shatters Mordred's army. Arthur and six others set out in pursuit of Mordred, who turns and makes a last stand by the sea-shore. After a severe battle, with the odds in Mordred's favour, only Arthur and Mordred are left. Mordred severely wounds his father, but is killed by him. Arthur's Helper appears for the last time and carries him to Avalon.

The epilogue turns first to Lancelot and Guinevere. Guinevere, having buried Arthur at Avalon, becomes a nun, but her love remains, and her tortured spirit never finds rest. She hears almost nothing from Lancelot until he sends Bors to her to say that he is dying. She arrives too late to see him, but his appearance in death overwhelms her: a weak old man with silver hair. 'I had not thought of him as old,' she says, and indeed she herself seems perpetually young. As he is buried, she thinks of her own death, which must soon follow, and feels that love at least will make her soul glimmer on, though all else be lost.

The last aspect of the story is that of Arthur as seen by later ages. First, Henry II's visit to the newly-discovered grave of Arthur gives us the point of view which says that Arthur is long since dead. But the apparently contradictory *On the Coming of Arthur* reveals that it is only his body that has crumbled to dust, while his spirit still lives on.

Finally, Masefield provides alternative versions of both the poems in which he has radically changed the story. *The Old Tale of the Begetting* begins:

> 'The men of old that made the tale for us
> Declare that Uther begot Arthur thus:'

In twenty-two lines he relates the old tale of transformation and magic, giving an unpleasant portrait of Uther. *The Old Tale of the Breaking of the Links* is longer: the introduction points out that the story of the abduction of Guinevere belongs to Tristram and Iseult, not Lancelot and Guinevere,* and says:

> '. . . but since men know
> This version best, I tell it also so.

The narrative that follows is in many ways more effective than Masefield's own version, but it is out of harmony with the rest of his cycle, and would not make a good substitute.

In this cycle, Arthur—for once—remains as the central figure of the story. It is always in relation to him that we see events, and there is never the separation of knights and king found in the French romances and works based on them. From the outset Badon Hill is regarded as the climax, and the pirates as Arthur's chief enemies. This is an almost historical view: yet Masefield has blended in the pseudo-history and romance versions as well. The former gives us the story of Uther and the last battle, the latter

* This is inaccurate: Chrétien de Troyes's *Chevalier de la Charrette*, the earliest work in which Lancelot appears, also involves the abduction story.

Morgause and Mordred's begetting, and Lancelot and Guinevere's love. Welsh legend has provided the character of Gwenivach and the basis for the *Sailing of Hell Race*. Layamon seems
to have supplied the supernatural element.

From this diverse mixture, Masefield has formed a united and
well-balanced story. It is that of Arthur himself rather than of
the Round Table, and it is Arthur's qualities and defects with
which it is concerned. The only unnecessary excursion into other
realms is that of *Venus and the Ring*. Otherwise, every poem ful-
fils a definite purpose; either it is part of the actual narrative or
an illustration of character. Excluding the duplicate versions,
the group of poems is in fact a perfect unity.

The characters are drawn from Welsh legend rather than
French. Arthur is the magnanimous and just king whose wisdom
is overwhelmed by forces greater than he can combat. Guinevere
and Lancelot seem to be fated to act as they do: Lancelot, after
killing the knights who had tried to surprise them, says:

> 'For I foresee the kingdom breaking
> 　Asunder from all this;
> Out of the welter of man's making,
> 　What must be is.'

They are agents of their own destruction: both love the King,
and yet cannot help but love one another. Lacheu, their son,
killed by the pirates, is in Welsh legend son of Arthur and
Guinevere. Gwenivach, 'the accursed', is directly from the
Welsh. Mordred, as with Lancelot and Guinevere, has no direct
precursor. Both the French and English characters of the name
are used. The story of his birth comes from the first, that of his
treachery from the second.

The verse provides a variety of tone throughout, although it is
always a type of ballad, for among the eighteen poems fourteen
metrical or stanzaic arrangements are used. Where the same one
is repeated, it seems to be intended as a link between the poems:
thus the essential elements of the story *The Birth of Arthur*, *The*

Begetting of Mordred, and *On the Coming of Arthur,* are connected by the same form. The two parts in which the pirates predominate, *The Taking of Morgause* and *Badon Hill* are in the same couplet metre, and the last Guinevere poems have three-line stanzas not used elsewhere. The ballad form is weak in that it may tend to bring out the unheroic and commonplace, especially in conversation.

Finally, Masefield's clarity of insight is remarkable. This is most apparent in the handling of the final tragedy: from *Midsummer Night* onwards, he reveals not only the effect but the inner feelings which cause it. Mordred's bitter outbursts, both in the poem of the title and in his final words—'Thirty years' anguish made by your idle lust': the helplessness of Lancelot and Guinevere after the fight on the wall: Arthur's joy in finding a new comrade in his son, and his reluctance to fight him when he is betrayed: the inextinguishable nature of Guinevere's love for Lancelot, and her eternal youth of spirit: all these touches tell us far more about the characters than the lengthy monologues of Chrétien de Troyes or Tennyson's didactic sermons, and as a result they seem more vital and energetic. Yet there is a certain lack of reality about the action, possibly because of the ballad metres used, and it is this that prevents it from ranking with Tennyson and Malory as a great expression of the legend, although the approach is better than either of these writers.

Masefield's handling of the Tristram theme is of an equally high standard. Again, for his play *Tristan and Isolt* (1927), 'he returns to the Welsh origins of the story': Arthur is a Romano-British general who seeks Mark's aid against the Saxons, and who is accompanied by Kai and Bedivere. Even the pig-stealing episode of the triads is brought in, if a little lengthily: Tristan is guarding the swine while their keeper goes on an urgent mission to Isolt.

The only real fault in the play, while its unity is good, is that the love motif is in the foreground too little of the time. National issues take precedence, although they are linked to the lovers' own history. Tristan releases Mark from vassalage to Kolbein by killing the latter, whose dying wish is that Mark should wed his daughter Isolt. As a result of Arthur's mission, Mark fights at Badon Hill, and is killed there. Tristan is beseeched on several occasions by his steward Dinan to leave Isolt and return to his kingdom.

Isolt is the most interesting character: when Mark discovers them sleeping in the forest and spares their lives, her immediate impulsive reaction is to return to him, an irrational but entirely natural move. Similarly, her refusal to see Tristan after Mark's death is equally impulsive and convincing. There is a humanity and warmth in Masefield's characters all too often abandoned by other writers for the sake of tragic grandeur, usually without any increased success.

The verse throughout is firm and appropriate, and has many poignant moments. Isolt, although her actual death scene is not as moving as it might be, delivers a beautiful speech as she goes to find the dying Tristan and kill herself:

'What shall I have?
Some sky for the two wild swans to be wing in wing,
Some holly thicket for the stag and his deer,
Some space in heaven, where I, the comet, will seek
My mate, past withering orbs and moons gone blind,
For centuries to come. I am following, Tristan;
Wait for your cruel killer, a little hour.
You shall be my death as I have been yours, beloved.
We who have flooded like the Severn, will ebb
To the great sea together like tides going out.'

Altogether, Masefield's contribution to the legend has been a large one, even if less well known and recognized than it should be. It may be that the personal style of his poems in a period when poets have sought to replace the personal and direct by the impersonal and obscure has hindered their fame.

·   ·   ·   ·   ·

At the opposite extreme of brilliance to Masefield's work stands the complexity of Charles Williams's conception of the Arthurian story, which, if highly personal, is certainly obscure. Contained in two volumes, *Taliessin through Logres* and *The Region of the Summer Stars*,[7] it is in essence, though not in detail, an extension of Tennyson's vision of Arthur as ideal man, for in Williams's poems Arthur's kingdom of Logres is to be the perfect union between earth and heaven. But the symbolism involved, though very moving, is intricate and difficult in the extreme. C. S. Lewis's exposition in *Arthurian Torso* is therefore invaluable, and the present writer could certainly never have compiled the following general outline of the poems and their meaning without its aid. But since it takes the poems individually, the plan of the whole cannot emerge clearly, and hence it may help those interested, as well as providing a basis for comparison with other poets, to have such an outline.

The poems are dominated by the concept of the Roman and Byzantine empires seen most clearly in *The Vision of the Empire*. The image is that of a reclining female figure. The 'skull-stone' is the rocky outer edge of Britain/Logres, which stands as the Empire's soul and brain. The breasts are in Gaul: the schools of Paris provide the nourishing milk of learning. On Rome the hands lie clasped: here the Pope says Mass with its 'heart-breaking manual acts'. Jerusalem is the womb, from which Adam, fallen man, came. Caucasia is the 'fool's shame', the bottom of the figure. Lastly there is Byzantium, the navel, in which all the 'dialects' arise and re-echo. These are the 'themes' of the Empire, which are related in the same way as the body.

There is an antithesis to the Empire, in P'o-Lu, where the headless Emperor of the Antipodes walks. This is the conseqquence of the Fall: bodies become shameful instead of a glory of creation, and so here the 'feet of creation' walk backwards. For in P'o-Lu are the feet of the Empire, and they are feet of clay. It is from here that the failure of Arthur's mission springs.

At the opposite extreme, beyond Logres, lies the Wood of

N

Broceliande—a sea-wood, Williams calls it—and beyond a certain part of it, Carbonek, the castle in which the Grail is kept.
Beyond this and a stretch of open sea, is Sarras, the home of the
Grail. This is Williams's most difficult concept; his deep religious and mystical feelings made it inevitable that a great deal of
both should occur in the poems, and this lies at the root of most
of it.

Through Broceliande lies the way from earth to heaven—as
witness the Grail city and castle. But Williams insists that these
last lie beyond only a certain part of it. If one goes far enough the
Antipodes may be reached through these same regions. C. S.
Lewis explains this apparent contradiction as follows:

> 'In a writer whose philosophy was Pantheistic or whose
> poetry was merely romantic, this formidable wood . . .
> would undoubtedly figure as the Absolute itself. . . . All
> journeys away from the solid earth are equally, at the outset,
> journeys into the abyss. Saint, sorcerer, lunatic and roman-
> tic lover, all alike are drawn to Broceliande, but Carbonek is
> beyond a certain part of it only. It is by no means the Abso-
> lute. It is rather what the Greeks called the Apeiron—the
> unlimited, the formless origin of forms.'

This then is the geography, physical and spiritual, of Williams's world. Against this background, Arthur, Taliessin and
Merlin work out their mission. Nimue, lady of Broceliande,
sends her children, Merlin and Brisen, to perform the great task
of perfect union. They meet Taliessin, the pagan poet of Wales
still, as they go to create the kingdom of balanced humanity, an
earthly kingdom like the holy kingdom of Carbonek, in which
the Empire and Broceliande, the physical, intellectual, and
spiritual, shall meet. Arthur is to be their instrument; they depart for Logres, and Taliessin for Byzantium.

Taliessin's part in the mission is difficult to grasp at once, but
we learn that on his return from Byzantium he bears with him
the vision of the Empire, standing for order, which he must

impose on the as yet chaotic Logres; this must be accomplished before the Grail can come to dwell there. He is also the type of the poet, which is bound up in his personal task. The poet, in Williams's view, is incapable of inspiring love for himself, yet can inspire others to it; this is illustrated in *Taliessin's Song of the Unicorn,* where the poet is likened to the unicorn, attracted to a virgin; she will not love him, and her lover will come and kill the unicorn out of jealousy.

Taliessin's mission is a success, and the Golden Age of Logres ensues. The lyric pieces which describe this involve many philosophical concepts, chiefly that of love. The last of these is *The Coming of Palomides*; Palomides looks on Iseult, sees the geometrical beauty of her form,* and dreams of the first kind of love, physical consummation. But as he looks, the Questing Beast

> '. . . scratched itself in the blank between
> The Queen's substance and the Queen.'

He must find the answer to the connection between the flesh and the spirit before he can find intellectual love.

But the plan as a whole is doomed to failure: the actual deeds which prevent Logres from becoming the kingdom of the Grail are Arthur's unwitting incest with Morgause, and Balin's equally unconscious slaying of his brother, and giving of the Dolorous Blow. Both pairs act blindly; it is not their individual fault that these things are done, but the fault of human nature, of fallen man. And deep below the surface of Logres, all is not going as it should.

Yet out of this failure springs a measure of success. The Grail cannot come to Logres; but the uncorrupted part of Logres may reach the Grail. It is again Taliessin's task to prepare the way. The company of his household are his instrument; at the base of their efforts lies salvation worked through poetry and the senses,

---

* Williams associates glory and beauty with geometrical patterns and rigid outlines; cf. Taliessin's analysis of the body in these terms in *Taliessin at the School of the Poets.*

Taliessin's own special task. The ideas here are too complex to be discussed in detail.

It is Taliessin as head of this 'Company of the Redeemed', who greets the first of the future Grail band to arrive at court—Percivale and his sister Dindrane.* Before the main action is continued, the structure of Taliessin's company with its three orders is expounded.

By the machinations of Merlin and Brisen, Galahad is born, at the cost of his father's sanity, for which Galahad later atones. He is delivered into Dindrane's charge to be cared for. One poem only fills the interval between this and his arrival at Court: *Palomides before his Christening*. Palomides has failed on his quest; intellectual love is not for him. But through disillusion-ment comes conversion—for until now he has belonged to the Moslem faith—even if it is only a belief in disbelief.

The coming of Galahad occurs on the evening of Palomides's christening, and we hear of it from Taliessin, Gareth and the slave, as they discuss it afterwards. One of the more important images here comes from Wordsworth's *Prelude*, Book V. The stone and shell borne by the Arab in this poem are fitted in Galahad; the union which was to have been Logres has been ful-filled in one man only. None save three will succeed, and reach Carbonek; the rest will sink into Britain. The forces of Broce-liande depart. Palomides finds the answer to his problem; what he had seen as ends in themselves, love, fame, irony, were only paths to a greater end, and, happy in this knowledge, he dies.

The climax and simultaneously the anti-climax is now reached. The Grail is achieved, but at the cost of Arthur's work, the Round Table. So triumph on the one hand, in *Percivale at Car-bonek*, and *The Last Voyage*, are balanced by the implied disaster of *The Meditation of Mordred* and *The Prayers of the Pope*. As the Grail is achieved, and withdrawn to Sarras, Logres sinks into the chaos out of which it had risen. Taliessin dissolves his com-pany, but they gather finally, in flesh or spirit, at the mass

---

* Or *Blanchefleur*. Williams seems to interchange the names freely.

performed by Lancelot. The mission has reached its end: all that could or can ever be achieved has been achieved. Lancelot's voice singing 'Ite; missa est' is the signal for the irrevocable dispersal, and 'that which was once Taliessin' rides slowly away.

The poems are in style their own worst enemies as far as enduring fame is concerned, since they are in the direct line of descent from the obscure references of *The Waste Land*, and much difficult philosophy is also involved. They require not merely notes but a complete commentary for even rudimentary comprehension. Yet the fact that they can hold the attention in spite of the formidable problem of even understanding them is a witness to their sheer poetic power. The verse is brilliant in its incantation, and the words flow and merge into a strange music. Here are two contrasting examples. Taliessin comes to Lancelot's mass at the end of the cycle:

'I came to his altar when dew was bright on the grass:
He—he was not sworn of the priesthood—began the Mass.
The altar was an ancient stone laid upon stones;
Carbonek's arch, Camelot's wall, frame of Bors' bones.

'In armour before the earthen footpace he stood;
On his surcoat the lions of his house, dappled with blood,
Rampant, regardant; but he wore no helm or sword,
And his hands were bare as Lateran's to the work of our Lord.'

But this is less typical of Williams than the following passage, the climax of Merlin's and Brisen's incantations at the launching of the mission:

'The stars vanished; they gone, the illumined dusk
Under the spell darkened to the colour of porphyry,
The colour of the stair of Empire and the womb of women,
And the rich largesse of the Emperor; within was a point,
Deep beyond or deep within Logres,
As if it had swallowed all the summer stars

And hollowed the porphyry night for its having and hiding—
Tiny, dark-rose, self-glowing,
As a firefly's egg or (beyond body and spirit,
Could the art of the king's poet in the court of Camelot,
After his journeys, find words for body or spirit)
The entire point of the thrice co-inherent Trinity
When every crown and every choir is vanished,
And all sight and hearing is nothing else.'

Williams has used the Arthurian legend as the mould for his
individual and intensely Christian philosophy. While the matter
and events of the old tales are retained, characters and values are
totally different. Yet in its obscure and mystical way this is one
of the great works of Arthurian literature. It is a heightening of
Tennyson's symbolism to the utmost, the spiritual application of
Swinburne's intense study of physical love in the frame of the
legend. When we are more used to such poetry—for whatever
may be claimed, such works are scarcely accepted and understood as yet—then Williams will come into his own.

To turn to T. H. White's novel, *The Once and Future King*,[8] is
somewhat of a mental relief. This is basically a modern retelling
of Malory, and, in its own way, a brilliant retelling. As the author
himself says: 'All the characters are the same, save that Pellinore
has a love-affair, and the fact that Lancelot is ugly.' But there is
one very important difference. To make the book less weighty,
while he still acknowledges it to be a serious matter, the author
has tempered the story with comedy. It is good comedy, with an
immediate appeal, such as has not been seen before in connection with Arthur. Whether this humour is very definitely of the
present day remains to be seen; if it is, it will be a great pity, for
it will reduce the book's chances of becoming an established
masterpiece for future generations, and White's exposition of
Malory is worth a dozen essays on the subject.

If this test is passed, the book can be regarded as a new
approach to the story. It is a Shakespearian tragedy, in which

the comedy sets off and heightens the tragedy. Malory provides the tragic material; White has developed it, and made the crux of the story a political and spiritual question, well put by Charles Williams in one of his Arthurian poems:

> 'The king made for the kingdom, or the
> kingdom made for the king?'

In Williams, Arthur gives the wrong answer, and this is partly why he fails, but here Arthur's education is entirely directed by Merlin to make him a king for the kingdom. Once again it is Mordred, the result of human weakness, who brings about his downfall, exploiting Lancelot and Guinevere's love to this end. The latter takes the place of Tristram and Iseult as the central love theme, and White's study of them is penetrating and fascinating.

The evocation of the England of the Middle Ages is again masterly, and far surpasses that of any other Arthurian writer to date. His knowledge of the subject is detailed and sure, and hence he can portray vividly anything from a hawking expedition and everyday life in a medieval castle to a full-scale siege. Such diverse information is put across entertainingly and in his usual pleasant style, which makes the book easy to read, a quality not common in Arthurian literature.

White's characters, which are the part of Malory's story that has undergone the most change, are entirely convincing. Sympathetically and occasionally humorously portrayed, Arthur is more real a human being here than he has been for a long while; for instance, his desperate struggle between duty and personal feeling when Guinevere is condemned to the stake is passed over in Malory with the words, 'and he was sore amoved', after which he acts impersonally as his duty directs. But in White, although he has to maintain his official position, he makes no secret of his hope that Lancelot will rescue the queen.

Nor are the minor characters mere names in the lists at tournaments. Gawain and his brothers are especially well depicted: the sullen Agravaine, gentle and loyal Gareth and Gaheris, and Mordred, their bitter, tortured half-brother. The comic characters are never stereotyped, even though they tend to belong to familiar groups—the old-school-tie knights, Pellinore and Grummor Grummorson, the pompous sergeant who teaches Arthur and Kay on the tilting-ground, with his waxed moustache and chest like a pouter-pigeon, Merlin in his lighter moments as an absent-minded magician—the list is endless but always varied.

The Once and Future King is certainly a masterpiece for our own time. It can only be hoped that its humorous side does not become dated, as has happened to *The Misfortunes of Elphin*, and that it does not slide into an undeserved oblivion as a result, for this is far more than comedy with tragic touches: in its own distinctive way, *The Once and Future King* realizes afresh the full force of what its writer himself calls 'the Aristotelian tragedy of Arthur'.

With this, our survey of Arthur's part in English literature comes to an end. But there remain some larger problems which have only been partially answered. Among these are the reasons for Arthur's dramatic reappearances, in the twelfth and nineteenth centuries, and the question of his relevance today. The immediate, factual answers have been outlined; yet there is something deeper than these.

The resurgences of Arthur in 1130 and 1830 are parts of larger movements in which he played an important part. In the twelfth century, the literatures and languages of modern Europe were just beginning to emerge. Latin, the normal language of any other than everyday matters, was beginning to retreat into the schools in face of the rising spirit of nationalism throughout the Continent. The Norse and Celtic countries alone possessed a vernacular literature of any size and interest, and contact between the two cultures was rare until the Normans invaded England. Here there existed a vernacular language of some standing, which was temporarily overwhelmed, and had less influence than those of the still independent peoples on the borders of the newly-conquered land. The Celtic races possessed what the Latin peoples lacked to a large extent—a popular epic repertoire with immediate appeal. It was only natural that when these tales, possessing admirable material inadequately exploited, reached the writers of the new vernacular by devious routes, they should be immediately adopted and used as poetic subjects.

But in England the problem was different: an already well-developed vernacular had been rendered useless for literary work of this sort, since the ruling classes spoke French. It was not until English began to be the language of all alike, that these new resources of literature could be exploited. Hence the appearance of the English works was tardy, and they obviously depended on the already abundant French stories. At first there was little demand for translations of a high standard, and the works were written by minstrels. The one major exception seems to have been commissioned by John of Gaunt. From this they sank to the level of popular ballads; and not until the merchants and squires took an interest in such matters, did a really adequate version appear, and even that was accompanied by several less inspired efforts.

In spite of Malory's magnificent achievement he was the end of a tradition as far as his subject was concerned, and before the onslaught of the new rationalist ideas the romantic side of Arthur and his fellows vanishes into the realms of mist from which it had come, and the remainder was thrown on the mercy of the historians. Here it shrank like Balzac's '*peau de chagrin*' until when Milton came to write his British epic he found there was nothing left.

But Arthur had at the end of the Middle Ages descended into folklore; and when folklore became a subject of curious interest among scholars at the end of the eighteenth century, he once more came to the notice of the poets. Gradually a revival of the legends started; but now there was no lack of themes as there

had been in the twelfth century, and it is harder to explain
Arthur's popularity in the last century, but there is no great
underlying cause. It has been a question of selection by individual poets as well as an instinctive movement towards him.
Tennyson and his contemporaries chose Arthur partly because
the tales about him had already been told in such a way as to fire
their imagination. But not only did they offer great possibilities
purely from the poetic point of view, but also a certain validity
for the time. England was triumphant abroad, mistress of a
growing empire, and national pride ran high. To this feeling the
stories of Arthur, a national hero, would have great appeal. The
rediscovery of Malory by Victorian readers had made the old
legends more familiar, and modern versions were bound to follow.

But had Tennyson failed to turn the legends into poetry with
such an immediate attraction to his generation, they might well
have remained a minor curiosity. The great bulk of the Arthurian plays and poems that followed between 1870 and 1900, is
evidently in imitation or emulation of him; Wagner's Arthurian
operas, especially 'Tristan und Isolde' are another major influence.

The notable exceptions are few, until a new reason for using
the Arthurian legend was found: its innate psychological drama.
Tennyson had exploited its moral side; but Swinburne heralds
the new exploration of the innermost depths of character. This
gave rise to the Arthuriana of the first quarter of the present century—works such as Symons's play and E. A. Robinson's poem
on Tristram and Iseult.

But in the last three works included, Masefield's *Midsummer
Night*, Charles Williams's *Taliessin through Logres* and *Region of
the Summer Stars*, and T. H. White's *The Once and Future King*,
we find the real answer to Arthur's present popularity among
writers. It is the diversity of the legends, which allows each to
choose material to his own taste. Masefield has taken the simp-
lest outlines of the story; Charles Williams its most difficult

concept, the Grail; and T. H. White, the comedy as well as the tragedy. Within the frame of the Arthurian story there is something that appeals to everyone.

Finally, we may ask what relevance the whole legend has for us today. We may feel that it is worth our attention because it offers human situations that are the same in every age; because the romances give us an insight into the medieval mind; because it reminds us of forgotten ideals which still have some value today. But there is one transcending and much simpler reason why the Arthurian legends will not be abandoned; and Caxton gave it five centuries ago: because in them we shall find 'many joyous and playsaunt hystoryes and noble and renomed acts of humanyte, gentylenesse and chyvalryes'. As long as English poetry is written, Arthur will be remembered; he may yet have many vicissitudes to come, but the legends are so intimate a part of our heritage that his figure will always emerge again, mysterious, heroic, and yet human.

APPENDIX A

SUGGESTIONS FOR FURTHER READING

FOR the reader who would now like to explore a little further the English works on Arthur, a few guiding remarks may be helpful. Working in chronological order, either Giles's or Sebastian Evans's translation of Geoffrey of Monmouth is the first recommendation, as being essential to the development of the stories, and in itself one of the more neglected masterpieces. If this is done, Wace and Layamon need not be considered, since they are too difficult, although excerpts from the latter are fascinating in small quantities. Of the romances, few are readily available. The *Morte Arthure* and *Sir Gawain and the Green Knight* embody all the best qualities, but neither is easy reading; there are several good modernisations of the latter. Percy's *Reliques* contain a few ballad fragments.

Malory would not be mentioned here, so obvious a choice is he, were it not that the usual texts have lately been shown to owe many alterations to Caxton. The Winchester MS. text, much closer in many respects to Malory's own, is available in the Oxford Standard Authors series, edited by Professor Vinaver, and well repays and slight extra trouble in obtaining it.

Of more recent writers, Tennyson needs no comment. Sir Walter Scott's *The Bridal of Triermain* is the best of his predecessors; William Morris's fragments in the first volume of the Longmans edition of his complete works and Swinburne's *Tristram of Lyonesse* make a very good contrast to the *Idylls*; while Arnold presents a view somewhere between the two schools. The writers of this century are the most numerous, and only a handful are really to be recommended. Masefield, both in *Midsummer Night* and the play *Tristan and Isolt* gives a lively and easily read account. E. A. Robinson's poems are the best yet to come from across the Atlantic; again the *Tristram* occupies pride of place. For those who are at home in modern mysticism and poetry, and are prepared to work to understand a poem, Charles Williams may seem the most distinguished author in the present list; but there will be no one who does not fall under the spell of T. H. White's *The Once and Future King*.

Critical works are more numerous than the texts for the medieval period, but the essence of most of them is distilled into *Arthurian Literature in the Middle Ages*, edited by R. S. Loomis. Otherwise, *Arthur of Britain* provides a more general view of the period. E. Vinaver's edition of Malory in three volumes is essential for that author. Modern works are covered by Maynadier's *Arthur of the English Poets* and N. C. Starr's lively account of this century's Arthur in *King Arthur Today*.

189

Appendix B

SELECTED BIBLIOGRAPHY

A: TEXTS AND TRANSLATIONS

CHAPTERS I–IV

Nennius and Gildas: ed. Camden Society, 1842. [Critical text.]

A. W. Wade-Evans (ed.): *Vitae Sanctorum Britanniae et Genealogicae* (University of Wales, 1944). [Some of the legends of the Welsh saints. Text and translation on facing pages.]

Sir E. K. Chambers: *Arthur of Britain* (Sidgwick and Jackson, London, 1927). [Some Latin texts are quoted at the end of the book.]

CHAPTER III

A. Griscom (ed.): *The Historia Regum Britanniae of Geoffrey of Monmouth* (New York, 1929). [The only text of the Vulgate version valid for critical purposes.]

J. J. Hammer (ed.): *Geoffrey of Monmouth. The Historia Regum Britanniae: A Variant Version* (Medieval Academy of America, Cambridge, Mass., 1951). [The Variant version texts are here given for the first time; only details are discussed.]

J. A. Giles: *Six Old English Chronicles* (Bohn's Standard Library, London, 1891). [Translations of Gildas, Nennius and Geoffrey of Monmouth, useful for reading and reference, but inadequate for critical purposes.]

S. Evans: *The Histories of the Kings of Britain* (Everyman's, 1912). [Again inadequate for critical purposes.]

L. A. Paton: *Arthurian Chronicles represented by Wace and Layamon* (Everyman's, 1912).

Sir F. Madden (ed.): *Layamon's Brut* (London, 1847).

M. M. Banks (ed.): *Morte Arthure* (London, 1900).

CHAPTER V AND VI

Continental works in translation

W. W. Comfort: *Arthurian Romances by Chrétien de Troyes* (Everyman's, 1914). [All Chrétien's works except the *Conte del Graal*.]

R. S. Loomis: *The Romance of Tristram and Ysolt* by Thomas of Britain (Columbia U.P., New York, 1951).

H. Belloc: *The Romance of Tristan and Iseult* (London, 1936). [From Bédier's version of Béroul.]

S. Evans: *The High History of the Holy Grail* (Everyman's, 1912). Translation of the French romance *Perlesvaus*. [Introduction on date and author not accurate.]

A. C. Hatto: Gottfried von Strassburg, *Tristan*, and Thomas, *Tristan* (Penguin, 1960).

J. L. Weston: *Parzival, A Knightly Epic by Wolfram von Eschenbach* (David Nutt, London, 1894).

English romances

J. Ritson (ed.): *Ancient English Metrical Romances* (London, 1802), 3 vols. *Ywain and Gawain* (I, pp. 1–169). *Sir Launfal* (I, pp. 169–215). *Sir Libeaus Desconus* (II, pp. 1–91).

J. D. Bruce (ed.): *Le Morte Arthur* (Early English Text Society, 1891).

J. Robson (ed.): *Three Early English Metrical Romances* (London, 1842). 'The Avowing of King Arthur', pp. 57–93.

Sir Walter Scott (ed. *et fin.*): *Sir Tristrem* (*Poetical Works*, vol. V, A. & C. Black, Edinburgh, 1880).

J. L. Weston: *Arthurian Romances unrepresented in Malory*, vol. V (London, 1902). [Translation of *Sir Libeaus Desconus*.]

J. L. Weston: *Chief Middle English Poets* (Boston, 1914). [Translations of *Sir Percyvelle of Galles* and *Sir Tristrem*.]

J. L. Weston: *Romance Vision and Satire* (Boston, 1912). [Translations of *Awntyrrs of Arthur* and *Sir Gawain and the Green Knight*.]

J. R. R. Tolkien and E. V. Gordon: *Sir Gawain and the Green Knight* (Clarendon, 1925).

B. Ford (ed.): *Guide to English Literature* (Penguin, 1953). [Text of *Sir Gawain and the Green Knight*.]

B. Stone (tr.): *Sir Gawain and the Green Knight* (Penguin, 1959).

Sir F. Madden (ed.): *Syr Gawayne, A Collection of Ancient English Romance Poems* (1839, Bannatyne Club). [All the Gawain romances, except *Ywain and Gawain*, accurately transcribed.]

Bishop T. Percy: *Reliques of Old English Poetry* (1777, Everyman's, 1912).

CHAPTER VII

E. Vinaver (ed.): *The Works of Sir Thomas Malory* (3 vols., Clarendon, 1947). [Text and full critical apparatus, including discussion of Malory's sources, differences between Caxton text and Winchester MS., etc.]

E. Vinaver (ed.): *The Works of Sir Thomas Malory* (1 vol., Oxford University Press, 1955, Oxford Standard Authors). [Text only of above with short preface.]

CHAPTER VIII

W. Hazlitt (ed.): *Dodsley's Old English Plays*, Vol. V ('The Misfortunes of Arthur').

B: CRITICAL WORKS

General up to 1485

Sir E. K. Chambers: *Arthur of Britain* (Sidgwick and Jackson, London, 1927). [Covers the early history, mythological and folklore aspects of Arthur clearly and fully. Little on subsequent developments. A useful introduction.]

R. S. Loomis (ed.): *Arthurian Literature in the Middle Ages* (Oxford, 1959). [A full and exhaustive treatment by thirty scholars of five nationalities; although now the standard work on the subject, is too technical for the ordinary reader.]

J. D. Bruce: *Evolution of Arthurian Romance to 1300* (2 vols., Göttingen, 1923–4, Hesperia Ergänzungsreihe, 8–9, rptd. New York, 1959). [None of the English romances falls within its scope, and it is largely replaced by Loomis's volume above. But it still remains one of the major Arthurian critical works.]

R. H. Fletcher: *The Arthurian Material in the Chronicles* (Harvard Notes and Studies, X, 1906). [Still in many ways the standard work on the pseudo-history of Arthur up to 1600 except for the section on Geoffrey of Monmouth has been superseded.]

J. P. S. Tatlock: *The Legendary History of Britain* (University of California, 1950). [More valuable for its mass of facts and details than for its general conclusions, which do, however, present the opposing view to that of Loomis.]

W. F. Schirmer: *Die frühen Darstellungen der Arthurstoffen* (Westdeutscher Verlag, Köln und Opladen, 1957). [A study of the literary and political aspects of Geoffrey of Monmouth, Wace and Layamon.]

R. S. Loomis: *Arthurian Tradition and Chrétien de Troyes* (Columbia U.P., New York, 1949). [This attributes to Chrétien less originality than had previously been credited to him, but explains many discrepancies. It is much more plausible in detail than previous theories of Celtic influence.]

R. S. Loomis: *Wales and the Arthurian Legend* (University of Wales, 1956). [A collection of articles related to Welsh influence on the legends, the last of which, 'The Arthurian Legend before 1139' is a valuable summary.]

CHAPTER I

O. G. S. Crawford: *Antiquity iv* (1935), p. 289. [King Arthur and his battles.]

R. G. Collingwood: *Roman Britain* (Bks. I–IV of Oxford History of England), pp. 320–4.

J. Lindsay: *Arthur and his Times* (F. Muller, London, 1958). [A good picture of Britain between 400 and 550.]

CHAPTER II

G. H. Gerould: *Speculum X* (1935), pp. 353–76. [Modena archivolt; evidence for late date.]

R. S. Loomis: *Speculum XIII* (1938), pp. 221–31. [Counter-evidence for early date.]

R. S. Loomis: *Wales and the Arthurian Legend.* Last chapter.

CHAPTER IV

J. Armitage Robinson: *Two Glastonbury Legends* (Cambridge U.P., 1926). [The most reliable work on the subject.]

L. S. Lewis: *St. Joseph of Arimathea at Glastonbury* (Clare and Co., Wells, 1937). [The opposite view to Robinson.]

G. Ashe: *King Arthur's Avalon* (Collins, London, 1955). [The borderline between fact and theory is too indistinctly drawn to make this book reliable.]

CHAPTER V

Miss J. L. Weston: *From Ritual to Romance* (Doubleday, New York, 1957). [The ideas on Celtic origins of the Grail do not correspond in more than the broadest outline to those held today.]

J. E. Wells: *A Manual of the Writings in Middle English 1050–1400* (Yale University Press, 1916), supplements 1919, 1923, 1926, 1929, 1932, 1935, 1938. [A comprehensive and reliable survey, including analyses of all the romances.]

CHAPTER VI

G. L. Kittredge: *A Study of Sir Gawain and the Green Knight* (Harvard, 1916). [Covers not only romance of the title but most of the other Gawain poems as well.]

B. Ford (ed.): *Penguin Guide to English Literature*, Vol. I. Chapter on Sir Gawain and the Green Knight.

CHAPTER VII

E. Vinaver (ed.): *The Works of Sir Thomas Malory* (3 vols., Clarendon, 1947). [Full critical apparatus.]

E. Vinaver: *Malory* (Oxford, 1929).

Sir E. K. Chambers: *English Literature at the Close of the Middle Ages* (Vol. II, Pt. II, of Oxford History of English Literature, 1945).

CHAPTERS VIII AND IX

R. F. Brinkley: *Arthurian Legend in the Seventeenth Century* (Baltimore, 1932). [Mainly concerned with the historian's view of Arthur.]

H. Maynadier: *The Arthur of the English Poets* (Cambridge, 1907). [First part a little outdated, but otherwise most comprehensive treatment to date. Excellent on period 1800–1900.]

M. Schüler: *Sir Thomas Malorys Le Morte D'Arthur und die englische Arthurdichtung des XIX Jahrhunderts* (Strassburg, Josef Singer, 1900). [Malory's influence on nineteenth-century writers; accurate but a little restricted in scope.]

M. J. C. Reid: *The Arthurian Legend: A Comparison of Treatment in Modern and Medieval Literature* (Oliver and Boyd, Edinburgh 1937; rptd. 1960) (A not entirely reliable assessment of Arthuriana in English from 1770–1930: useful for reference).

N. C. Starr: *King Arthur Today*. (University of Florida Press, 1954). [A readable and thorough account of the better works of this century.]

APPENDIX C

GENEALOGIES

GENEALOGY OF ARTHUR ACCORDING TO GEOFFREY

Aurelius Ambrosius   Uther Pendragon (2) —— Igerna (1) —— Gorlois

Guanhumara —— Arthur   Urian   Augusel   Lot (2) —— Anne (1) —— Dubricius

Hoel

Mordred   Walgan

An alternative reading would give:

Dubricius —— daughter   Aurelius Ambrosius   Uther Pendragon (2) —— Igerna (1) —— Gorlois

Hoel

Guanhumara —— Arthur   Anne —— Lot

Mordred   Walgan

This confusion arises out of two different references in Geoffrey's work as to Anne's husband. He cites both Dubricius and Lot on different occasions (VIII 21, IX 2, IX 9).

GENEALOGIES ACCORDING TO MALORY

(1) *Arthur*

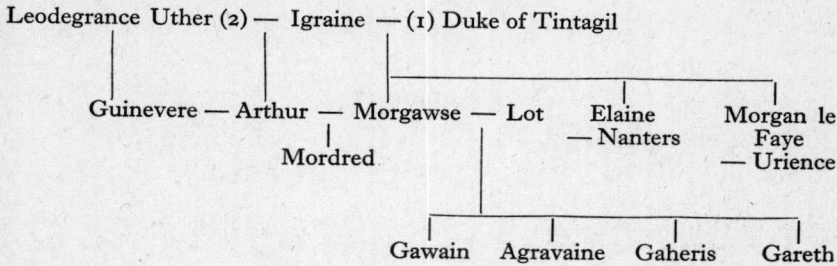

(2) *Lancelot*

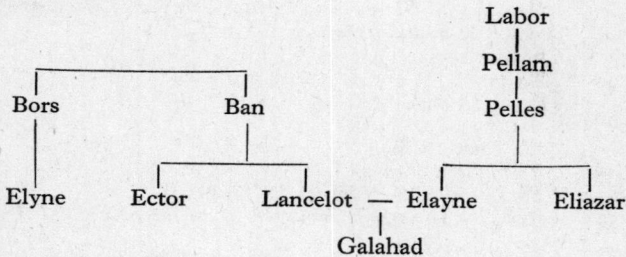

(3) *Tristram*

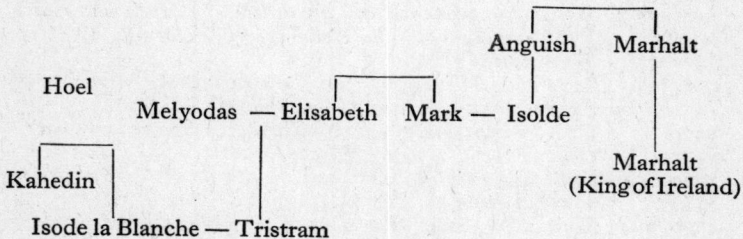

Appendix D

A: CHRONOLOGICAL LIST OF ENGLISH ARTHURIAN LITERATURE

KEY: (pr) prose work; (p) poem; (d) drama; (tr) tragedy; (n) novel. Important continental works or writers are included. These are marked *.

1135	Geoffrey of Monmouth, *Historia Regum Britanniae* (pr).
1155	Wace, *Roman de Brut* (p).*
1165	fl. Chrétien de Troyes.*
c. 1190	Layamon, *Brut* (p).
1200–30	Prose Vulgate Cycle completed.*
1250–1300	*Arthour and Merlin* (p).
1290	*Sir Tristrem* (p).
1300–50	*Ywain and Gawain* (p).
1325–50	*Sir Launfal, Sir Libeaus Desconus* (p).
c. 1350	*Avowing of Arthur, Awntyrrs of Arthur, Joseph of Arimathie* (p).
1350–1400	*Sir Percyvelle of Galles, Alliterative Morte Arthure, Arthur* (p).
c. 1370	*Sir Gawain and the Green Knight* (p).
1375–1400	Stanzaic *Le Mort Arthur* (p).
1400–1500	*Sir Gawain and the Carl of Carlisle, The Turk and Gawain, The Green Knight, The Wedding of Sir Gawain, The Gest of Sir Gawain* (p).
c. 1450	Lovelich's *Merlin and Holy Grail* (p), *Prose Merlin*.
1450–1500	*Golagros and Gawane, Sir Lancelot du Laik* (p).
1470	Sir Thomas Malory, *Morte Darthur*, original form (pr).
1485	Caxton's edition of the *Morte Darthur*.
1510	*Little Tretys of the Birth and Prophecies of Merlin* (pr.)
1587	Thomas Hughes, *The Misfortunes of Arthur* (tr).
1590–6	Edmund Spenser, *The Faery Queen* (p).
1610	Richard Johnson, *Romance of Tom a Lincolne* (pr).
1612	Michael Drayton, *Polyolbion* (p).
1640	Martin Parker, *History of Arthur* (pr).
1691	John Dryden, *King Arthur* (opera; music by Purcell).
1695	Sir Richard Blackmore, *Prince Arthur* (p).
1697	Sir Richard Blackmore, *King Arthur* (p).
1777	Thomas Warton, *Grave of King Arthur* (p).
1804	Sir Walter Scott, edition and completion of *Sir Tristrem* (p).

1809	Sir Walter Scott, *The Bridal of Triermain* (p).
1829	Thomas Love Peacock, *Misfortunes of Elphin* (n).
1830	William Wordsworth, *The Egyptian Maid* (p).
1832	Tennyson, *Lady of Shalott* (p).
1842	Tennyson, *Sir Launcelot and Queen Guinevere, Sir Galahad, Morte d'Arthur* (p).
1848	Lord Lytton, *King Arthur* (p).
1858	William Morris, *The Defence of Guinevere* and other poems.
1859	Tennyson, *Idylls of the King I* (p).
1863	R. S. Hawker, *Quest of the Sangreal* (p).
1865	Wagner, *Tristan und Isolde*.*
1869	Tennyson, *Idylls II* (p).
1880	J. R. Lowell, *Sir Launfal* (p).
1882	Swinburne, *Tristram of Lyonesse* (p).
1885	Tennyson, *Idylls III* (p).
1891	R. Hovey, *Lancelot and Guinevere* (d).
1895	J. Comyns Carr, *King Arthur* (d).
1896	Swinburne, *Tale of Balen* (p).
1898	J. Davidson, *The Last Ballad* (p).
1911	Michael Field, *Tragedy of Pardon, Tristan de Leonois* (tr).
1913	Laurence Binyon, *Tristram's End* (p).
1917	Arthur Symons, *Tristram and Iseult* (tr).
1923	Hardy, *The Queen of Cornwall* (tr).
1925	T. S. Eliot, *The Waste Land* (p).
1927	Masefield, *Midsummer Night* (p), *Tristan and Isolt* (tr).
1928	E. A. Robinson, *Tristan* (p).
1938	Charles Williams, *Taliessin through Logres* (p).
1944	Charles Williams, *The Region of the Summer Stars* (p).
1948	Charles Williams—C. S. Lewis, *Arthurian Torso*.
1958	T. H. White, *The Once and Future King* (n).

B: CHRONOLOGICAL TABLE OF THE CHRONICLES CONCERNING ARTHUR

KEY: l—Latin, f—French, e—English, v—verse.

1135	Geoffrey of Monmouth, *Historia Regum Britanniae* (l).
1155	Wace, *Roman de Brut* (fv).
1190	Layamon, *Brut* (v).
1290	*Robert of Gloucester* (v); Anonymous short chronicle (v).
1307	Peter Langtoft (fv).
c. 1325	Thomas Castelford (v).
1338	*Robert Mannyng of Brunne* (v).
1385	Fordun, *Chronica Gentis Scotorum* (l).
1420	Wyntoun, *The Original Chronykil of Scotland* (v).
c. 1430	Capgrave.
1436	Hardyng (v).
c. 1450	*Arthur* (Bath MS.) (v).
1511	Fabyan, *New Chronicles of England and France*.

1521   Mair, *History of Great Britain* (l).
1527   Boece, *Scotorum Historia* (l).
1534   Polydore Vergil, *Anglicae Historiae*, xxxiv (l).
1562   Grafton, *Abridgement of chronicles of England.*
1565   Stow, *Abridgement of English chronicles.*
1577   Holinshed.
1580   Stow, *Chronicles of England.*
1586   Warner, *Albion's England.*
1613   Drayton, *Polyolbion.*

APPENDIX E

NENNIUS'S ACCOUNT OF ARTHUR

THERE are such wide variations in the manuscript texts that it was thought that a full account of these would be useful. The basic text is that of Harleian MS. 3859, of the tenth century, translated from the Camden society edition, as are the variants. MS. A is in the Vatican Library, is contemporary with the Harleian one, and possibly more reliable. The rest are lettered according to age:

B—Cotton Caligula, A, viii (Brit. Mus.), *c.* 1150.
C—Cotton Nero, D, viii (Brit. Mus.), *c.* 1200.
D—Corpus Christi College Cambridge, cxxxix, thirteenth century.
E—Burney MS. (Brit. Mus.), 1381.
m denotes a marginal addition in any of the above.

In those days the Saxons grew in numbers and prospered in Britain. But at Hengist's death, Octha his son came from the western parts of the island to the kingdom of Kent, and from him sprang the kings of Kent. Then Arthur[1] and the kings of the Britons fought against them, but Arthur himself was leader of the battles.[2] The first battle was at the mouth of the river called Glein:[3] the second, third, fourth and fifth on another river, which is called Dubglas,[4] in the region Linnuis.[5] The sixth battle was on the river known as Bassas.[6] The seventh was in the forest of Celidon, that is to say, Cat Coit Celidon.[7] In the eighth battle at Castle Guinnion,[8] Arthur bore upon his shoulders[9] the image of Mary, the Holy Virgin; the heathen were put to flight that day, and through the might of our Lord Jesus Christ there was a great slaughter of them. The ninth battle took place at the City of Legions.[10] The tenth battle was waged on the banks of the river Tribroit.[11] The eleventh

[1] A: Arthur the warrior.
[2] A, D, m: Although there were many more noble than he, he was twelve times commander and victor in the battles.
[3] C: Gem. C, m: Glem.
[4] A, C: Duglas.
[5] B, m: Lindsey.
[6] A: Lusas.
[7] A: Cacoit Celidon. C: Catoit Celidon.
[8] A: He fought the eighth battle against the barbarians near a castle.
[9] Here an emendation to all MSS. has been suggested, since the Welsh iscuit (shield) and iscuid (shoulders) might easily have been confused by a translator. However, the *Annales Cambriae* also read shoulders; an error would have to be in a common source.
[10] B, m: which the British call Kairliun.
[11] B: Ribroit. C: Robroit. B, m: Trathtruiroit.

battle was fought on the mountain called Agned.[1] At the twelfth battle on Mount Badon, there fell in one day nine hundred and sixty men[2] under one onslaught of Arthur's men, and none conquered save he alone, and in all the battles he was victor.[3]

[1] A: which we call Cat Bregion. B: Agned Cathbregomion. B, m: Bregion in Somersetshire, which we call Cathbregion. C: Agned Thabregomion. C, m: Agned Cathbregonion.

[2] E: 840.

[3] D adds: Arthur went to Jerusalem, and there made a cross from a piece of the True Cross, which was consecrated in the same place: he spent three days in vigil and fasting before the Cross of our Lord, praying that God would give them victory over the pagans by this token, which indeed happened. And he took with him the image of the Virgin Mary, the fragments of which are preserved in great veneration at Wedale. D, m: Wedale in English is Vallae Doloris in Latin, a town in the province of Lothian, in the bishopric of St. Andrews, six miles to the west of that noble monastery of Melrose. (Wedale is now identified with Stow, near Melrose.)

BIBLIOGRAPHICAL NOTES

Throughout these notes certain standard works are referred to a number of times, and to reduce the length involved the following abbreviations have been used. For further details as to date, publisher and content, see 'Bibliography'.

ALITMA—*Arthurian Literature in the Middle Ages*, ed. R. S. Loomis.
ATCT—*Arthurian Tradition and Chretien de Troyes*, R. S. Loomis.
Chambers—*Arthur of Britain*, by Sir E. K. Chambers.
Fletcher—*The Arthurian Material in the Chronicles*, by R. H. Fletcher.
Giles—*Six Old English Chronicles*, translated by J. A. Giles.
Griscom—*Historia Regum Britanniae*, ed. A. Griscom.
Hammer—*A Variant Version of the Historia Regum Britanniae*, ed. J. J. Hammer.
Maynadier—*The Arthur of the English Poets*, by H. Maynadier.
Reid—*The Arthurian Legend: A Comparison of Modern and Medieval Treatments*, by M. J. C. Reid.
Starr—*King Arthur Today*, by N. C. Starr.
Tatlock—*The Legendary History of Britain*, by J. P. S. Tatlock.
Vinaver 1947—*The Works of Sir Thomas Malory* (3 vols.), ed. E. Vinaver (Clarendon, 1947).
Vinaver 1955—*The Works of Sir Thomas Malory* (1 vol.), ed. E. Vinaver (O.U.P., 1955).
Wales—*Wales and the Arthurian Tradition*, by R. S. Loomis.

CHAPTER I

[1] R. G. Collingwood and J. N. L. Myres, *Roman Britain and the English Settlements*. J. Lindsay, *Arthur and his Times*.
[2] Edited for the Camden Society, 1842; translation, J. A. Giles, *Six Old English Chronicles*.
[3] *De Excidio Britanniae*, chap. 25–6. Giles, pp. 312–13.
[4] Collingwood and Myres, op. cit., pp. 460   ff.
[5] Chambers, pp. 262–3.
[6] Giles, p. 314. ff.
[7] Giles, p. 295.
[8] *Canu Aneirin*, ed. Ifor Williams (Cardiff, 1938), pp. xiv ff. Quoted by K. H. Jackson, ALITMA, p. 3.
[9] H. M. and N. K. Chadwick, *Growth of Literature* (Cambridge, 1932), i, pp. 146–66.
[10] Cf. Geoffrey of Monmouth, *Historia Regum Britanniae*, chap. 19–20. Giles, pp. 224–6.
[11] Collingwood and Myres, op. cit., pp. 464 ff., and J. Lindsay, op. cit., pp. 216–17. But see also K. H. Jackson, ALITMA, p. 9, who dismisses it without even discussing the theory.

CHAPTER II

[1] *Nennius*, ed. Camden Soc., 1842, ch. lxxiii; and Chambers, pp. 239–40.
[2] K. H. Jackson, ALITMA, p. 14.
[3] *Wales*, pp. 131–78.
[4] Lady C. Guest, *The Mabinogion*, London, 1838.
Studies: *Wales*, pp. 191–2.
      I. L. Foster, ALITMA, pp. 31–9.
      Tatlock, pp. 194–9, for opposing view.
[5] I. L. Foster, ALITMA, p. 38.
[6] R. Bromwich, ALITMA, pp. 44–51.
[7] Giraldus Cambrensis, *De Instructione Principum* (*Opera* ed., Brewer and Dimock, Rolls Series, viii, p. 127). See also chap. 4.
[8] See also ch. 5.
[9] R. S. Loomis, *The Romance of Tristan and Isolt*, preface.
[10] A. W. Wade-Evans, *Vitae Sanctorum Britanniae et Genealogicae*, pp. 26–8, 68–70. Chambers, pp. 81, 245–6.
[11] Chambers, pp. 82–3, 246–7.
[12] Tatlock, pp. 193 ff.
[13] Chambers, pp. 84–5; ATCT pp. 214–9; *Wales*, pp. 182–3.
[14] Chambers, pp. 262–4.
[15] See chap. 4.
[16] Giles, p. 89.
[17] R. S. Loomis, ALITMA, pp. 60–1; *Wales*, pp. 199–208.
G. H. Gerould (against early date) *Speculum X*, 1935, pp. 355–76.
R. S. Loomis (in answer to above) *Speculum XIII*, 1938, pp. 221–31.
J. P. S. Tatlock (against early date) *Legendary History of Britain*, p. 214.
[18] Gerould, loc. cit., p. 357.
[19] *Wales*, pp. 208–13; Tatlock, pp. 222–6 for opposite view.
[20] R. S. Loomis, ALITMA, p. 61.

CHAPTER III

[1] Editions: Griscom, Hammer (Variant Version).
Translations: Giles. [Not reliable for critical purposes.]
      S. Evans, *The Histories of the Kings of Britain* Everyman's, 1912). [Not used.]
[2] Tatlock, pp. 396–402, supports the latter.
[3] Giles, p. 89; Hammer, p. 22; Griscom, p. 219.
[4] Giles, pp. 194–5; Hammer, p. 123; Griscom, pp. 383–4.
[5] Chambers, p. 274.
[6] Giles, pp. 402–3.
[7] Giraldus Cambrensis, *Opera* (ed. Brewer and Dimock, Rolls Series, 1867), vi, p. 216.
[8] A. O. H. Jarman, ALITMA, chap. 3.
[9] Griscom, pp. 42–96.
[10] R. A. Caldwell, *Bulletin bibliographique de la société internationale arthurienne*, no. 9, p. 123.
[11] J. J. Parry and R. A. Caldwell, ALITMA, p. 81.
[12] Giles, p. 234; Hammer, pp. 154–5, 228; Griscom, p. 438.

[13] R. S. Loomis, ATCT, pp. 423–5.
[14] Giles, p. 268; Hammer, pp. 186, 250; Griscom, p. 496.
[15] Giles, p. 236; Hammer, pp. 157, 230; Griscom, p. 443.
[16] J. Rhys, *Celtic Folklore*, Oxford, 1903.
[17] Tatlock, p. 314.
[18] Tatlock, chap. xx.
[19] Giles, p. 237; Hammer, pp. 157, 230; Griscom, p. 443.
[20] Tatlock, pp. 270–4; Giles, pp. 242–5; Hammer, pp. 162–5, 234–7; Griscom, pp. 451–8.
[21] Tatlock, chap. xiii.
[22] Chambers, p. 274.
[23] Tatlock, pp. 450–6.
[24] Wace, *Roman de Brut*, ll. 15297–15300.
[25] Layamon, *Brut* (ed. Madden, London, 1847), pp. 41–4.
[26] Faral's edition in *La Légende Arthurienne*, Paris, 1929, iii, pp. 63–303.
[27] ATCT, pp. 59–67.
[28] R. S. Loomis, ALITMA, p. 105.
[29] Layamon, *Brut*, ll. 18533–28651.
[30] Schirmer, Die frühen Darstellungen des Arthurstoffes, pp. 65–8.
[31] Fletcher, pp. 151–5, gives additions and omissions.
[32] ATCT, pp. 62–7.
[33] ATCT, p. 55.
[34] British Museum, Cotton Caligula, A, ix, and Cotton Otho, C, xiii.
[35] G. Neilson, *Notes and Queries*, Series IX, vol. X, pp. 161–5, 301–3, 402–4. *The Antiquary*, Aug. 1902.
[36] Fletcher, pp. 193 ff.

Chapter IV

[1] Ed. N. K. Chadwick, *Studies in Early British History* (Cambridge, 1954), p. 112.
[2] K. H. Jackson, ALITMA, p. 13.
[3] Hermann of Laon, *De miraculis S. Mariae Laudunensis* (1146), ii. Quoted Chambers, p. 249.
[4] William of Malmesbury, *De Rebus Gestis Regum Anglorum* (Rolls Series), ii, p. 342.
[5] Fletcher, p. 107, n. 7, for all chronicle treatments of Arthur's return.
[6] Alanus de Insulis (Alan of Tewkesbury), *Prophetia Anglicana Merlini Ambrosii Britanni*, I, p. 17, quoted Chambers, p. 265.
[7] Giraldus Cambrensis *Opera* (ed. Brewer and Dimock, Rolls Series, 1867), viii, p. 126.
[8] Ralph of Coggeshall, *Chronicon Anglicanum*, quoted Chambers, p. 268.
[9] Giraldus Cambrensis, op. cit., iv, p. 47.
[10] Bishop Ussher, *Antiquitates* (ed. 1687), p. 63.
[11] Adam of Domerham, *Historia de Rebus Gestis Glastoniensibus* (ed. T. Hearne, 1727), p. 341.
[12] Caradoc of Llancarfan, *Vita Gildae*, quoted Chambers, pp. 262–3.
[13] ATCT, p. 219.

204 ARTHUR OF ALBION

14 Chambers, pp. 221–5.
15 Dean Armitage Robinson, *Two Glastonbury Legends* (Cambridge, 1926), p. 53.

CHAPTER V

1 ATCT, pp. 7–10.
2 J. Frappier, ALITMA, pp. 158–61.
3 See translation by W. W. Comfort, Everyman's Library, pp. 91 and 865.
4 H. Newstead, ALITMA, p. 122.
5 E. Vinaver, *Works of Sir Thomas Malory* (Oxford, 1947), p. 1267.
6 For general remarks on the English romances see R. Ackerman and J. N. O'Loughlin, ALITMA, pp. 480–3, 520–1, and D. Everett, 'A Characterisation of the English Mediaeval Romances', *Essays and Studies by Members of the English Association* (xv, 1929).
7 R. Ackerman, ALITMA, pp. 485–6.
8 Ibid., pp. 488–9.
9 Ibid., pp. 486–8.
10 Ibid., 499–500.
11 J. N. O'Loughlin, pp. 509–11, and ATCT, p. 335.
12 J. L. Weston, *From Ritual to Romance*, and *Legend of Sir Perceval*.
13 A. C. L. Brown, *Modern Philology*, 1919–21, vol. 16, pp. 553–; 17, pp. 361–; 18, pp. 201–, and 661–. *The Grail and the English Sir Percyvelle*.
14 J. D. Bruce, *Evolution of Arthurian Romance to 1300*, Göttingen, 1923, II, chap. viii.
15 R. Ackerman, ALITMA, pp. 519–20.
16 G. Schöpperle, *Tristan and Isolt*, a study of the sources of the romance, Frankfurt, 1913. J. D. Bruce, op. cit.
17 See R. S. Loomis's and Hilaire Belloc's translations.
18 R. Ackerman, ALITMA, p. 514–16, and Walter Scott, *The Romance of Sir Tristrem* (Edinburgh, 1819).
19 R. Ackerman, ALITMA, pp. 491–3.
20 Ibid., pp. 489–91.
21 J. D. Bruce, op. cit., I, p. 449; *Anglia*, xxiii, pp. 75–97 and edition for EETS (1903).
22 R. Ackerman, ALITMA, pp. 512–14.
23 S. McHugh, *Modern Philology*, 1945, vol. 42, pp. 197–. 'Celtic parallels for Sir Libeaus Desconus'.
24 See chap. 7 and J. Wilson, PMLA, 1943, 58, pp. 1–22. 'Malory and the Fair Unknown'.
25 R. Ackerman, ALITMA, pp. 516–18.
26 J. D. Bruce, op. cit., I, p. 60, and E. Hoepffner, ALITMA, pp. 118–19.

CHAPTER VI

1 L. H. Loomis, ALITMA, pp. 527–40.
2 *Cotton Nero*, X (British Museum).
3 W. Oakden, *Alliterative Poetry in Middle English*, Manchester, 1935.
4 B. Stone, *Sir Gawain and the Green Knight*, Penguin, 1959, Appendix 2.

5 Kittredge, pp. 38–40, 66–7.
6 Kittredge, p. 295. J. R. Hulbert, *Modern Philology*, vol. xiii, pp. 433–.
7 B. Stone, op. cit., Appendix 6.
8 R. Ackerman, ALITMA, pp. 497–8.
9 Ibid., pp. 496–7.
10 Kittredge, pp. 274–81.
11 R. Ackerman, ALITMA, pp. 494–5.
12 A. Buchanan, PMLA, vol. 47, pp. 331–.
13 Kittredge, pp. 257–73.
14 R. Ackerman, ALITMA, pp. 501–5.
15 Ibid., pp. 507–9.
16 J. L. Weston, *Modern Languages Quarterly*, 1899, vol. 2, pp. 98–, 194–.
17 ATCT, p. 269.
18 R. Ackerman, ALITMA, p. 500.
19 J. N. O'Loughlin, ALITMA, p. 527.
20 Percy's *Reliques* (Everyman's ed.), II, p. 211.
21 Ibid., vol. II, p. 404.
22 Ibid., vol. I, p. 196.
23 Ibid., vol. II, p. 205.
24 R. Ackerman, ALITMA, p. 498.
25 Ibid., pp. 518–19 and Percy's *Reliques*, II, p. 188.
26 Vinaver, 55, p. 327.

CHAPTER VII

1 A. C. Baugh, *Speculum*, vol. vii, p. 4.
2 Vinaver, 1947, pp. xxxvi–xl.
3 Vinaver, 1947, pp. 1387–9.
4 Vinaver, 1955, pp. 180–9, 189–96, 196–209.
5 Vinaver, 1947, pp. 1400–1.
6 Vinaver, 1947, pp. 1417–9.
7 Vinaver, 1955, p. 623.
8 J. Donaldson, *Studies in Philology*, 1950, vol. 47, pp. 460–73. 'Malory and Le Mort Arthur.' Vinaver, 1947, p. 1572.
9 Vinaver, 1955, p. 194.

CHAPTER VIII

1 Dodsley's *Old English Plays*, ed. W. Hazlitt (London, 1873–4), pp. 248–343.
2 In Chalmers's *English Poets* (London, 1802), vol. XVIII.
3 Schüler, pp. 23–7; Maynadier, pp. 335–9; Reid, pp. 42–3.
4 Schüler, pp. 40–3; Maynadier, pp. 348–50; Reid, p. 44.
5 Schüler, p. 40; Maynadier, pp. 344–8; Reid, pp. 111–13.
6 Schüler, pp. 64–8; Maynadier, pp. 351–2; Reid, pp. 39–40.
7 Schüler, pp. 60–4; Maynadier, pp. 383–9; Reid, p. 240.
8 Schüler, pp. 81–125 (sources, pp. 90–113); Maynadier, pp. 410–38; Reid, *passim*.
9 Tennyson, *Idylls of the King*, ed. Hallam, Lord Tennyson (London, 1908), p. 438.
10 Vinaver, 1955, pp. 58–70.

[11] Vinaver, 1955, p. 73.
[12] Vinaver, 1955, pp. 123–6.
[13] Vinaver, 1955, pp. 860–73.
[14] Schüler, pp. 50–60; Maynadier, pp. 357–63; Reid, pp. 91–2, 96–100.
[15] Vinaver, 1955, pp. 791–3.
[16] Schüler, pp. 136–45; Maynadier, pp. 369–75; Reid, pp. 211–19.
[17] Schüler, pp. 70–6; Maynadier, pp. 363–5; Reid, pp. 141–3.
[18] Maynadier, pp. 379–82; Reid, pp. 144–5.
[19] Maynadier, pp. 406–9; Reid, pp. 102–4.
[20] Maynadier, pp. 397–404.

CHAPTER IX

[1] Reid, pp. 220–3; Starr, pp. 16–18.
[2] Reid, pp. 231–6; Starr, pp. 58–60.
[3] Reid, pp. 241–3; Starr, pp. 72–83.
[4] Reid, pp. 51–8, 104–7; Starr, pp. 40–1.
[5] E. K. Chambers, *Arthur of Britain*, pp. 185–95 and 220–30, deals with such legends.
[6] Reid, p. 236; Starr, pp. 61–6.
[7] Starr, pp. 166–78, and C. S. Lewis's commentary in *Arthurian Torso* (O.U.P., 1948).
[8] Starr, pp. 45–50, 115–24.

INDEX

P

Ygerne (*see* Igerna), 170
York, 38
Yorkshire, 20, 21
Yvain, 91
Yvain, see Chrétien de Troyes

Ywain (Owein ap Urien, Yvain, Ivan, knight), 17, 23, 74, 78, 86, 111–16
Ywain and Gawain, 81, 89 111–14